Elementary School Principals in Action

Other Books by the Author

SLAA Crash Course: Approaches for Success (2017)
Improving Instructional Practice: Resolving Issues in Leadership through Case Studies
    (2017)
Reflective Practice: Case Studies for Secondary School Principals (2018)

Elementary School Principals in Action

Resolving Case Studies in Leadership

Wafa Hozien

ROWMAN & LITTLEFIELD
Lanham • Boulder • New York • London

Published by Rowman & Littlefield
A wholly owned subsidary of The Rowman & Littlefield Publishing Group, Inc.
4501 Forbes Boulevard, Suite 200, Lanham, Maryland 20706
www.rowman.com

Unit A, Whitacre Mews, 26-34 Stannary Street, London SE11 4AB

British Library Cataloguing in Publication Information Available

Library of Congress Cataloging-in-Publication Data

Name: Hozien, Wafa, author.
Title: Elementary school principals in action : resolving case studies in leadership / Wafa Hozien.
Description: Lanham : Rowman & Littlefield Publishing Group, Inc., [2018] | Includes bibliographical references.
Identifiers: LCCN 2017024784 (print) | LCCN 2017045015 (ebook) | ISBN 9781475836424 (electronic) | ISBN 9781475836400 (hardcover : alk. paper) | ISBN 9781475836417 (pbk. : alk. paper)
Subjects: LCSH: Elementary school principals—United States—Case studies. | Educational leadership—United States—Case studies.
Classification: LCC LB2831.92 (ebook) | LCC LB2831.92 .H79 2018 (print) | DDC 372.12/012—dc23
LC record available at https://lccn.loc.gov/2017024784

♾ ™ The paper used in this publication meets the minimum requirements of American National Standard for Information Sciences Permanence of Paper for Printed Library Materials, ANSI/NISO Z39.48-1992.

Printed in the United States of America

For my children because they had to sacrifice as much as I did.
For Hana, the oldest and brightest of them all.
For Ismail, the nurturer of my spirit.
For Isra, who is, without fail, always here for me.
For Mahmoud, whose spirit resonates with all who meet him.
Thank you all for being in my life.

Contents

Introduction   ix

1 On a Schooling Mission   1
2 Instructional Leadership and School Improvement   29
3 Multicultural Issues and Cultural Competence   51
4 Human Resource Management   81
5 Family and Community Engagement   115
6 Case Study Resolutions   131

About the Author   155

Introduction

Today, in order to meet the needs of all students so they learn at high levels, principals must be more skilled than ever before. According to Sergiovanni (2005), principals must reflect on teaching and learning needs, set expectations, collaboratively develop visions for their schools, do strategic planning, and communicate goals for their schools to the school community. They must not only be able to help improve student achievement but also respond to the needs of all stakeholders, include them in the decision-making process, and empower them to take action.

This book views the principalship as a social role in a complex social organization. Leadership involves far more than simply certifying oneself in easily defined skills and tasks. It is a complex social process in which authority must be socially and morally earned. This approach to the principalship is the timeliest since today's principals are responsible for the overall operation of their schools. Some of their duties and responsibilities are delineated in state statutes, and states and school districts have set expectations for principals through their principal evaluation criteria and procedures.

During the latter part of the twentieth century, as schools began to be held more accountable for the performance of their students on national and state assessments, the duties and responsibilities of principals changed. Principals became more responsible for teaching and learning in their schools.

In particular, their duty to monitor instruction increased along with their responsibility to help teachers improve their teaching. With this change in responsibilities, principals discovered the need to more effectively evaluate instruction and assist teachers as they worked to improve their instructional techniques. The principal's duty to improve the school instructional program is mandated by legislation in some states, which often requires the removal of principals when schools are classified as low performing, meaning students do not meet achievement expectations for a specified period of time.

PRINCIPAL DUTIES AND RESPONSIBILITIES

The role of the public school principal is to create a learning environment that provides high-quality educational programming and instruction for students, regardless of their economic circumstances and in spite of strong correlations between socioeconomic status and academic performance (Jenlink, 2000). Principals' actions have a direct impact on the instruction that teachers provide, and elementary school principals in particular have a more significant role in instructional leadership than their high school principal peers (Sergiovanni, 2005). Principal leadership has been found to indirectly affect student achievement mainly through its impact on classrooms and teacher practices.

With schools facing increased pressure to improve teaching and learning, the duties and responsibilities of principals expanded further to include the responsibility for leading school reform to raise student achievement. Success in leading this type of reform often hinged upon a principal's ability to create a shared vision within the school community and success in implementing new organizational structures to engage teachers in shared decision making. Principals have discovered that engaging the entire school staff in making decisions results in more commitment to school-reform initiatives.

Principals are also responsible for facilitating their school's interactions with parents and others in the school community. This includes working with parents when disciplinary issues arise, when students are not succeeding academically, and when parents have concerns. Principals also interact with parents who serve on school advisory boards, in parent-teacher organizations, and in booster clubs. Principals report that they spend a significant part of their time working with parents of students who have been identified as needing special services through the Individuals with Disabilities Education Act Amendments of 1997 (IDEA).

Principals continue to be responsible for the management of their schools even though their primary responsibility has shifted. One major management responsibility is school safety in the age of the smartphone. This means that technology must be used appropriately and to increase student achievement.

The responsibility for school safety also includes the assurance that facilities and equipment are safe and in good working order, the development of overall school discipline policies and the enforcement of those policies, and the assignment of supervisory responsibilities among school personnel. At the elementary level, principals are cognizant of their responsibility to ensure constant supervision of the very young children in the school.

PRINCIPAL QUALIFICATIONS

A license is required for those who seek employment as principals in most states. Licensure requirements vary from state to state, but the requirements generally include experience as a teacher, graduation from a state-accredited principal-preparation program, and a passing score on a nationally validated licensure exam. Some states, like California and Texas, have their own content-specific exams (Hozien, 2017a). Principal qualifications were the subject of considerable debate during the 1990s and still are today as pressure increases to make schools more accountable for student achievement.

National organizations representing principals and other school administrators have actively engaged in the debate over appropriate qualifications for principals. In the mid-1990s the National Policy Board for Educational Administration (NPBEA) decided to review principal qualifications. The NPBEA included most of the major national organizations that represent education administrators, from state superintendents to principals, as well as organizations that represent professors who prepare school administrators. One of the members, the Council of Chief State School Officers (CCSSO), took on the major role of developing a set of standards for school leaders.

Working with the member associations and representatives from thirty-seven states, the CCSSO led the effort to identify a new set of standards for principals. This group was known as the Interstate School Leaders Licensure Consortium (ISLLC). Today the NPBEA is taking a leading role in updating the standards for principal certification.

This book is aligned with the ten standards, rewritten by the NPBEA in 2015, that were designed to influence the preparation of principals, guide states in the development of their own statewide principal standards, and serve as a tool for licensure or evaluation (Hozien, 2017a). The descriptors accompanying the standards have been omitted here for the sake of brevity. The ten standards address a principal's need to promote the success of all students through the following:

Standard 1. Mission, Vision, and Core Values
Standard 2. Ethics and Professional Norms
Standard 3. Equity and Cultural Responsiveness
Standard 4. Curriculum, Instruction, and Assessment
Standard 5. Community of Care and Support for Students
Standard 6. Professional Capacity of School Personnel
Standard 7. Professional Community for Teachers and Staff
Standard 8. Meaningful Engagement of Families and Community
Standard 9. Operations and Management
Standard 10. School Improvement

The 2015 standards are meant to be a guide for states and leadership-preparation programs as they identify and develop the specific knowledge, skills, dispositions, and other characteristics required of educational leaders to achieve real student success in school.

These standards became the basis upon which universities rely in educating future school leaders. A number of states use the Educational Testing Service–developed School Leaders Licensure Assessment (SLLA), along with other criteria, to license principals (Hozien, 2017a).

ROLE OF THE SCHOOL LEADER

Beginning in 1977, Senate committee reports have emphasized the importance of leadership, asserting that the principal is the most important and influential individual in a school (U.S. Department of Education, 2014). Researchers have linked effective school leadership with higher levels of student achievement; hence, it is important to understand the responsibilities of the principal when schools are undergoing a standards-based reform (Marzano, Waters, McNulty, 2005).

While there is no common definition of school leadership, Northouse (2013) has defined leadership as a process by which an individual influences a group of people to achieve a common goal. The role of the principal is complex and has many dimensions; however, ensuring student growth and student progress is paramount. Furthermore, the role of the principal becomes crucial with federal policies mandating, and annually measuring, student achievement outcomes (Northouse, 2013; U.S. Department of Education, 2014).

According to Kouzes and Posner (2007), "leadership is not about personality; it's about behavior" (p. 15). Since the early 1980s, Kouzes and Posner have studied the conditions that must exist in order to promote "personal-best leadership" (p. 14). They identified five practices of exemplary leadership: model the way, inspire a shared vision, challenge the process, enable others to act, and encourage the heart. In this book, using a case-study format, I identify practices and leadership qualities found in school leaders who have successfully served some of the most marginalized and vulnerable students.

When principals actively lead to change school conditions related to governance structure, school culture, school-wide policies about retention, adherence to the curriculum, and working conditions for teachers, variations in student achievement may occur (Leithwood and Steinbach, 1995). We know that principals have a substantial impact on assessment scores.

Significant changes in education require the principal to bring about a successful transition to new systems. According to Fox (2003), "Regardless of the type or impetus for change, the principal plays a key role in any restructuring efforts" (p. 5). Fullan (2014) stated, "The key to the speed of quality change is embedded in the power of the principal helping to lead organization and system transformation" (p. 10).

According to Syed (2013), "Effective principals work hard to improve the quality of instruction in their schools, through steps including observing teachers at work in the classroom, giving them detailed feedback, and providing them with the right professional development" (p. 32). This is at the heart of this book: bringing about crucial conversations to lead the future school principal toward continuous improvement.

This book is written on the premise that the important roles of the principal affect student achievement and describes what effective school leadership looks like. An effective school leader produces change by establishing direction, aligning people, and then motivating and inspiring them (Northouse, 2013). There are many types of leaders (all of whom may be effective) from servant leaders, who desire to help others, to instructional leaders, who provide resources and instructional assistance, communicate clear goals, and maintain high visibility during the school day (Marzano, Waters, and McNulty, 2005).

One of the newest areas of leadership—authentic leadership—describes a leader who is genuine or "real," a person who is transparent and exhibits interpersonal skills (Northouse, 2013). Though there are many different types of leaders, some people believe that individuals are born with specific leadership traits; others believe that leadership can be learned (Northouse, 2013). The latter is the more widely held view. Keep this in mind as you set out to resolve the case studies in this book and ask the questions:

- What style of school leader will I be?
- What kind of school environment do I want to create?

Marzano, Waters, and McNulty (2005) posit that school leaders are charged with twenty-one responsibilities that are directly linked to positive student academic achievement. Twelve of the twenty-one responsibilities should be shared with and delegated to a strong leadership team; however, in order to establish a purposeful school community, the other nine responsibilities should be held by the school leader (Marzano, Waters, and McNulty, 2005). The nine responsibilities of the principal are:

- optimization
- affirmation
- ideals/beliefs
- visibility
- situational awareness
- relationships

- communication
- culture
- input

Furthermore, change is accomplished by involving all staff in a shared vision led by the school principal. Principles of change are crucial to a school principal's ability to implement new programs. According to Fullan (2014), "The key to the speed of quality change is embedded in the power of the principal helping to lead organization and system transformation" (p. 10). Leaders must know which changes to make and which not to make (Knapp et al., 2014). This is imperative, especially with the introduction of the Common Core State Standards (CCSS) and the renewed focus on instructional leadership.

According to Syed (2013), effective school principals establish a school-wide vision with high expectations and a commitment to all students. Principals must communicate with teachers and parents. Principals ensure that their school is safe and supportive and that a sense of community exists. Additionally, principals should encourage leadership throughout the school staff. Principals should understand the curriculum standards. Strong principals are good managers and utilize data to identify student characteristics and areas where support is needed for success to occur (Syed, 2013).

McLaughlin, Glaab, and Carrasco (2014) explained, "School leaders must support their teachers as they make these transitions, while engaging parent and community members in new ways" (p. 1). For change to occur in education, the school must be open to change. Additionally, the school must have the capacity to change, with all stakeholders committed to change.

The responsibilities of contemporary principals have increased dramatically, and principals continue to be held accountable for school-improvement efforts. Leading the school-improvement process is a daunting task. Elementary school principals across the United States have reported that they consider helping teachers increase student learning to be a high leadership priority for school improvement. Principals should have this goal at the heart of all school-improvement efforts and make it a leadership priority.

However, data indicates that elementary school principals spend more time on management or administrative responsibilities than on helping teachers improve student performance (Robertson, 2006). This book, through the case studies presented, examines the numerous and diverse responsibilities of the principalship and the contexts in which elementary school principals work. It scrutinizes the various ways that principals make decisions that lead to effective education practices, thereby allowing the future principal to manage a school so that it runs smoothly and simultaneously to lead school-improvement efforts by helping not only teachers but all stakeholders to increase student learning.

INCREASED DEMANDS FOR ACCOUNTABILITY

The perceived failure of our public schools has resulted in an overloaded improvement agenda. An increased awareness of the importance of the principal to all change efforts, coupled with research that consistently points to the individual school as the focus of change and improvement (Goodlad, 1994; Sarason, 1982; Sinclair and Ghory, 1997; Tyler, 1992), has increased the pressure on principals to improve schools.

Principals are expected to lead the simultaneous implementation of an ever-increasing number of initiatives and mandates (Evans, 1997). The responsibilities of elementary school principals have become much more challenging, numerous, and diverse, and many principals "worry about ending up in the position of a manager of a baseball team that is losing; in most cases, the manager goes and the players stay" (Conley, 1993, p. 83). In most states, principals are held personally accountable for improving student achievement and have reason for concern. Furthermore, principals who lead schools determined to be underperforming according to statewide achievement tests run the risk of losing their professional license.

Nationwide, numerous mandates have been handed down, and principals are being held responsible for improving schools (Hozien, 2017b) because the NPBEA wrote the school leadership proficiencies to now include organizational management and fiscal management based on program goals and objectives, as well as political management that reflects an understanding of the dynamics of local, state, and national political pressures.

The standards were released with principles of effective administrative leadership in which indicators and their accompanying descriptors for leadership are now part of the increased scrutiny of school leaders. The principles are organized into ten broad categories followed by a description of the responsibilities. A review of these principles with its indicators and descriptors reveals the diverse responsibilities of the principalship. To increase school leadership proficiency and successful school practices, this book is aligned to the ten standards that were revised by the NPBEA in 2015.

FEATURES OF THE TEXT

In order to prepare for a future in educational leadership, readers will benefit from analyzing cases that represent different problems from a myriad of school types. The point of this book is not just to resolve cases but to show that respect for others is a moral principle indispensable for administrators. This is an admitted bias, one that undergirds both multicultural education and social justice emphases.

Along these same lines, administrators owe as much to the gifted and talented as to the intellectually and behaviorally challenged, as much to girls as to boys, and as much to one ethnic or religious group as to another. More specifically, all students and professionals deserve every opportunity possible to reach their respective degrees of excellence. These are commitments necessitated by the concepts in the case studies presented here, which help define the profession.

To bring people together into conversation requires a thoughtful and focused effort by all constituents and a commitment to understanding diversity in all its forms, including social and moral ones. Still, as educators, we know and appreciate the importance of keeping things simple whenever possible. Principals in effective schools consistently demonstrate a commitment to school improvement. Most important, this vision brings coherence and integration to school planning by the entire school community through the stewardship of the school leadership team.

This book has accompanying instructional resources that can be accessed from its Rowman & Littlefield website page, https://rowman.com/ISBN/ 9781475836400/Elementary-School-Principals-in-Action-Resolving-Case-Studies-in-Leadership. Select the Features tab and then click on the link. The case studies in this book have been abridged there and therefore made for online teaching. The purpose is to allow professors to use these case studies in their online courses. Students can read case studies prior to coming to class, then the instructor can place a condensed version in a PowerPoint presentation or a document to share with the class to facilitate class discussion.

Most school principalship texts are filled with the necessary components of knowledge building. These books have the required latest research and findings that build a foundation for the school principalship. To emphasize the focus on practice throughout this book, I use the pedagogical device of the case study to stimulate immediate reflection on an important idea or issue as it appears in the text. Students resolve the case studies in class by answering the questions at the end. To make this easier for students and instructors, I split each chapter into the following sections and placed the resolutions to the case studies in chapter 6:

1. Title
2. Background
3. Issue
4. Dilemma
5. Questions

Title: It is important to know the subject matter and, then, the school-leader standard this case study references and uses.

Background: This is the setting designed to prompt collaboration and shared understanding with others engaged in reading the same material. This exposes the text to a greater variety of criticism, and I believe everyone can benefit from such moments of focused dialogue.

Issue: Here the key points are identified: a compilation of items relevant to the case study.

Dilemma: Consider the information you do and do not have. Consider and assess the possible solutions before moving on to the questions.

Questions: This technique stimulates extended reflection about issues always and centrally close to the heart of the subject matter. The reader is asked to weigh the situation.

Resolutions: Identify a proposed strategy before reading this section, which has the main findings and recommendations. Suggested solutions are aligned to the 2015 Professional Standards for Educational Leaders (PSEL), previously known as ISLLC.

Online Instructional Resources: Abridged versions of all the case studies are found online on the Rowman and Littlefield site. These condensed versions of the cases are important for professors of education leadership who teach online.

As indicated by Hozien (2017b), readers can use the following as a formulaic guide to resolving case studies:

What issues are at stake here?
What should the school leader do?
If necessary, create a step-by-step short-term/long-term action plan.
What would you hope your action or decision accomplishes?
What possible risks or downsides are there to your action or decision?

ORGANIZATION OF THIS BOOK

This book consists of three sections. The first (chapters 1 to 5) has the actual case studies aligned to the latest school leadership standards. The second (chapter 6) has the possible resolutions for these case studies. They are provided in case the reader has missed an aspect of the case study in trying to resolve it. The third is the online abridged version of the case studies. Online instructional resources are provided for readers (see the previous page).

This book is further divided into five chapters dealing with the core content that future educational leaders will deal with:

Chapter 1: On a Schooling Mission
Chapter 2: Instructional Leadership and School Improvement
Chapter 3: Multicultural Issues and Cultural Competence
Chapter 4: Human Resource Management

Chapter 5: Family and Community Engagement

Each case study in this book offers a different background with a unique problem to solve. Depending on the specifics of the case, it is possible that the most significant components are in a combination of the paragraphs presented.

An important note: readers are encouraged to conduct appropriate research and investigate district, state, and federal mandates that relate to each case to develop a responsible foundation for analyzing the cases and solving the problems presented. As future educational leaders, it is up to you to meet the challenge of effective school leadership. This book is a learning aid that reminds the reader that, in the end, the goal is always to seek application to the realities of the school setting and the district.

The organization of this book is based on PSEL (2015). Each chapter is aligned to two or more standards, depending on the case study that is being resolved. The alignment to the standards for each case study is indicated in its title, as shown here:

Chapter 1: On a Schooling Mission. Standard 1—Mission, Vision, and Core Values; Standard 2—Ethics and Professional Norms

Chapter 2: Instructional Leadership and School Improvement. Standard 4—Curriculum, Instruction, and Assessment; Standard 10—School Improvement

Chapter 3: Multicultural Issues and Cultural Competence. Standard 3—Equity and Cultural Responsiveness; Standard 5—Community of Care and Support for Students

Chapter 4: Human Resource Management. Standard 6—Professional Capacity of School Personnel; Standard 9—Operations and Management

Chapter 5: Family and Community Engagement. Standard 7—Professional Community for Teachers and Staff; Standard 8—Meaningful Engagement of Families and Community

The table on the next page shows the matchup of all the case studies in this book with their corresponding PSEL standard.

Case Studies Arranged by PSEL (2015) Standard

STANDARD	CASE STUDY
1. Mission, Vision, and Core Values	• Duty Schedules • Survey Insights • Workroom Whispers • Viral Video • Not in My School
2. Ethics and Professional Norms	• Viral Video • Fifth-Grade Follies • Sticks and Stones • Because I Said So • Not in My School
3. Equity and Cultural Responsiveness	• Ticket to Fun • Rainy Day Recess • Bullying on the Bus • Sanctuary School • Not in My Classroom
4. Curriculum, Instruction, and Assessment	• Data Matters • Story Time • More Than a Day on a Calendar • Someone Like Me • A Failure of Leadership
5. Community of Care and Support for Students	• Someone Like Me • Bullying on the Bus • Left Behind • Restroom Pass • The Red Sweater • The Field Trip
6. Professional Capacity of School Personnel	• Social Media Mavens • Custodial Calamity • Time for Professional Development
7. Professional Community for Teachers and Staff	• Restroom Pass • Legendary Lothario • I Gotta Be Me • Same Old, Same Old • Don't Drink the Water
8. Meaningful Engagement of Families and Community	• Not in My School • Rainy Day Recess • Restroom Pass • The Field Trip • Stroller Moms • Where's My Kid? • When Push Comes to Shove
9. Operations and Management	• Playing Possum • A Failure of Leadership

	• High Mobility, Low Tolerance
	• When It Rains, It Pours
	• Stroller Moms
	• Celebratory Gunfire
10. School Improvement	• Flu Epidemic
	• They Read Just Fine
	• Change Begins Now
	• Where's My Kid?

BIBLIOGRAPHY

Brown, K. M., Benkovitz, J., Muttillo, A. J., and Urban, T. (2011). Leading schools of excellence and equity: Documenting effective strategies in closing achievement gaps. *Teachers College Record* 113(1): 57–96.

Common Core State Standards Initiative. (2012). *Standards in Your State*. Retrieved from http://www.corestandards.org/standards-in-your-state/.

Conley, D. T. (1993). *Roadmap to Restructuring: Policies, Practices and the Emerging Visions of Schooling*. Oregon: ERIC Clearinghouse on Educational Management.

Dewing, R., Perini, M. J., and Silver, H. F. (2012). *The Core Six: Essential Strategies for Achieving Excellence with the Common Core*. Alexandria, VA: Association for Supervision and Curriculum Development.

Evans, R. (1997). *The Human Side of School Change: Reform, Resistance, and the Real-Life Problems of Innovation*. San Francisco: Jossey-Bass.

Fox, S. L. (2003). Leading with change principles (doctoral dissertation). Available from ProQuest Dissertations and Theses database (UMI No. 3114709).

Fullan, M. (2014). *The Principal: Three Keys to Maximizing Impact*. San Francisco: Jossey-Bass.

Goodlad, J. I. (1994). *What Schools Are For*. Los Angeles: Phi Delta Kappan.

Hozien, W. (2017a). *SLLA Crash Course: Approaches to Success*. Lanham, MD: Rowman and Littlefield.

Hozien, W. (2017b). *Improving Instructional Practice: Resolving Issues in Leadership through Case Studies*. Lanham, MD: Rowman and Littlefield.

Jenlink, P. M., ed. (2000). *Marching into a New Millennium*. Lanham, MD: Scarecrow.

Knapp, M. S., Honig, M. I., Plecki, M. L., Portin, B. S., and Copland, M. A. (2014). *Learning Focused Leadership in Action: Improving Instruction in Schools and Districts*. New York: Routledge.

Kouzes, J. M., and Posner, B. Z. (2007). *The Leadership Challenge*. (4th ed.). San Francisco: Jossey-Bass.

Leithwood, K. A., and Steinbach, R. (1995). *Expert Problem Solving: Evidence from School and District Leaders* (SUNY Series, Educational Leadership). Albany: State University of New York Press.

Marzano, R. J. (2003). *What Works in School: Translating Research into Action*. Alexandria, VA: Association for Supervision and Curriculum Development.

Marzano, R. J., Waters, T., and McNulty, B. (2005). *School Leadership That Works from Research to Results*. Alexandria, VA: Association for Supervision and Curriculum Development.

McLaughlin, M., Glaab, L., and Carrasco, I. H. (2014). *Implementing Common Core State Standards in California: A Report from the Field*. Palo Alto, CA: Policy Analysis for California Education (PACE). Retrieved from http://edpolicyinca.org/publications/implementing-Common-Core-State-Standardscalifornia-Report-Field.

National Association of Elementary School Principals. (2008). *Leading Learning Communities: Standards for What Principals Should Know and Be Able to Do*. Reston, VA: Author.

National Association of Secondary School Principals (2014). *Breaking Ranks: 10 Skills for Successful School Leaders.* Reston, VA: Author.

Nelson, S. W., and Guerra, P. L. (2013). Educator beliefs and cultural knowledge implications for school improvement efforts. *Educational Administration Quarterly* 50(1): 67–95.

Northouse, P. (2013). *Leadership Theory and Practice.* (6th ed.). Thousand Oaks, CA: Sage.

Robinson, V., Lloyd, C., and Rowe, K. (2008). The impact of leadership on student outcomes: An analysis of the differential effects of leadership types. *Educational Administration Quarterly* 44(5): 635–74.

Robertson, P. (2006). *How Principals Manage Their Time.* National Association of Elementary School Principals. Retrieved from http://www.naesp.org/resources/2/Principal/2006/N-Dp12.pdf.

Sarason, S. (1982). *The Culture of the School and the Problem of Change.* Boston: Allyn and Bacon.

Sergiovanni, T. J. (2001). *The Principalship: A Reflective Practice Perspective.* (4th ed.). Boston: Allyn and Bacon.

Sergiovanni, T. J. (2005). *Strengthening the Heartbeat: Leading and Learning Together in Schools.* New York: Sage.

Seyfarth, J. (1999). *The Principalship: New Leadership for New Challenges.* Upper Saddle River, NJ: Merrill.

Sinclair, R. L., and Ghory, J. (1997). *Reaching and Teaching All Children.* Thousand Oaks, CA: Corwin Press.

Syed, S. (2013). Leading schools through major change. *Principal Leadership* 14(2): 30–33.

Thoonen, E. E., Sleegers, P. J., Oort, F. J., Peetsma, T. T., and Geijsel, F. P. (2011). How to improve teaching practices: The role of teacher motivation, organizational factors, and leadership practices. *Educational Administration Quarterly* 47(3): 496–536.

Tyler, R. W. (1992). *Improving School Effectiveness.* Amherst, MA: Coalition for Equality in Learning.

Ubben, G., et al. (2001). *The Principal: Creative Leadership for Effective Schools.* (4th ed.). Boston: Allyn and Bacon.

U.S. Department of Education. (2014). Elementary and Secondary Education Act. Retrieved from http://www.ed.gov/esea.

Youngs, P., and King, M. B. (2002). Principal leadership for professional development to build school capacity. *Educational Administration Quarterly* 38(5): 643–70.

Chapter One

On a Schooling Mission

—◦◦◦—

1. Duty Schedules

Grade Level: Suburban Elementary School, Grades PK–5
Standard: 1c, Mission, Vision, and Core Values

2. Background

Lisa Ennis was about to begin her third year as the principal of Eagleton Elementary. By working diligently to hire the best staff and teachers she could find, Ms. Ennis had a roster of competent educators who, she felt, would become educational leaders as their careers progressed.

To help her teachers experience leadership at a variety of levels, Ms. Ennis implemented a variety of initiatives not being carried out at the other campuses in the district. One example concerned the duties of the grade-level chairperson. Traditionally, staff at each grade level in the district's elementaries assisted with that grade level's particular needs. The grade-level chairpersons would assist their teams with reminders about deadlines for posting grades, by locating instructional resources, and by sharing teaching tips with new teachers.

There was no additional pay associated with the title of *chairperson*, but being selected for the position was considered an honor and a sign of respect. Usually, the most experienced teachers held these positions.

Ms. Ennis, however, wanted to provide an opportunity for every teacher to learn leadership skills, so she reassigned the grade-level chairperson role to a new teacher every six weeks. Rotating the title and the duties gave each teacher in the grade level an opportunity to step forward and learn new skills.

The most experienced teachers took the title in the beginning of the year so that newer teachers could learn the ropes before their turn arrived.

The initiative was successful. Each grade-level chairperson helped the next one take on the duties that came with the role, and the teachers learned a good deal about themselves and what it took to be a good leader. Some loved the opportunity to lead others, while other teachers did not, but they could appreciate the work of others.

With this strategy a success, Ms. Ennis decided to try another strategy that would invite teacher ownership in the operation of the school and again hone their leadership skills.

When the teachers arrived at the beginning of the school year, they would be encouraged to set their own schedules within the parameters set by state law regarding minutes of instruction and the district's requirements. Ms. Ennis provided each grade level with the following information:

- copies of the schedules from the previous two years
- state requirements for minutes of instruction per subject each week
- district requirements for teaching each subject
- start and end times for the school day
- class rosters for each teacher

The teachers were directed to devise their grade-level instruction schedules, include a conference period in their day, and arrange for students to attend a "special"—either art or music. The grade-level teams also had to set up a duty schedule for themselves, with coverage of student areas in the morning, at lunch, and after school.

Principal Ennis realized that the scheduling meant that the teachers would have to collaborate within their teams and across grade levels. She was eager to see how it would all play out.

"I'll be in my office if you need help," the principal told her teachers.

The morning passed slowly, with teachers coming through the office to grab another cup of coffee or a donut or a piece of fruit before going back to work on the instructional and duty schedules.

Just before lunch, however, tempers flared up. The third-grade teachers left as a group, arguing and slamming doors. The first-grade teachers followed them, also in hurry. The third-grade teachers came through one at a time, choosing not to go out to lunch together, and the office staff didn't see any of the other teachers.

Ms. Ennis decided that she needed to meet with all the teachers when they returned from lunch. She told her office staff to notify the teachers that she would meet with them when they returned from lunch.

Ninety minutes later, Ms. Ennis stood in front of her teachers in the cafeteria, where they had been working on the schedules.

"Okay, what do you have so far?" she asked the teachers.

"A mess. That's what we have," said one of the second-grade teachers. "We want to have our conference period right after lunch, but the fourth-grade team says that's *their* time slot. Fifth grade wants it, too."

"We only want that conference period because it fits nicely with our lunch. We have the toughest group discipline-wise, so we deserve to have our conference period next to our lunchtime. Lunch and conference back to back means we can go off campus and eat out."

"That's not fair," said one of the kindergarten teachers. "You're thinking of yourselves when you ought to be thinking of the kids. Our kindergarteners need an early lunch and late recess, or they will fall asleep in class."

"But it's our turn to get a good schedule," said one of the third-grade teachers. "You always get your way. We have small children of our own and want last-period conference so we can pick them up on time from day care."

As Ms. Ennis looked at the schedules submitted by each team of teachers, she noticed that they all wanted their conference periods first period, last period, or right after lunch. In addition, each team chose the easiest duty stations, and no one could agree on which special classes the students would take or when.

"I thought you were ready to take this on," said Ms. Ennis. "I am afraid I failed you."

3. Issue

Principal Ennis wanted to develop leadership skills in her teachers, and in the past, she had developed successful initiatives that helped teachers learn to take charge as they stepped into leadership roles.

Ms. Ennis's latest initiative was to allow the grade-level teams to develop their own instructional schedules rather than her doing it for them. She felt they were ready to collaborate with one another on a larger scale than usual. She tasked the teachers with arranging their instructional and duty times in collaboration with all the teams across the campus.

The teacher teams selected the same time slots for their conference periods and the optimal locations for duty. Most of the teachers arranged their instructional schedules for their convenience rather than for student needs. The teachers were unable to agree on mutually beneficial schedules.

4. Dilemma

Because the teachers were unable to build instructional schedules on their own, Ms. Ennis now has to step in resolve disputes and set the instructional schedule for each grade level. That means Ms. Ennis will have to build the master schedule and plan conferences and duty periods for her teachers, but more importantly, she will have to create instructional schedules that meet student needs first and foremost.

She will also have to help her teachers move beyond their frustration and get along with one another again. The teachers lost a day of professional development that could have been better spent on instructional planning.

5. Questions

1. What did the statement "I am afraid I failed you" say about Ms. Ennis?
2. What needs to be in place for the teachers to successfully meet the scheduling requirements?
3. Why did the teachers not do well with writing their own instructional schedules?
4. How would the schedules be different if they had kept child-development needs in mind? Which grade level should get preferred time slots for their conference periods?
5. How can Ms. Ennis resolve the issue of teacher frustration? Suggest specific ways to resolve conflict.
6. What are other ways Ms. Ennis could encourage teacher leadership?

1. Survey Insights

Grade Level: Urban Elementary Charter School, Grades PK–5
Standards: 1b, f, Mission, Vision, and Core Values

2. Background

Mike Michaelson had every intention of involving his faculty in the mission, vision, and goal setting for their campus, Best Charter Elementary. He wanted to be the kind of principal who valued the input of his teachers. After all, no one knew what students needed in the classroom better than the teachers working with them.

Mr. Michaelson had already been talking to teachers about what they were seeing, and many of the teachers seemed to be on target. The principal was impressed that teachers were concerned more about student welfare than their own, but he wanted to send out a comprehensive survey to verify his hunches and determine areas of strengths and weaknesses that he hadn't thought about.

The survey would go to every teacher and staff member. He also wanted to send it to the parents of his students, as well as community leaders and stakeholders. He envisioned central office and the school board taking his survey as well.

Principal Michaelson selected the survey for his campus. It was one he had used before from a national organization whose work was well respected in education. With seventy-five questions, it was a long survey, but it delved into the professional standards for educational leaders and would present a comprehensive analysis of campus strengths and weaknesses.

The teachers at Best Charter Elementary were eager to take the survey and see the results. However, Mr. Michaelson's project was delayed after he attended a meeting with the other principals and the superintendent.

The superintendent, Rory Richards, had heard about Mr. Michaelson's intentions to send out a campus survey. Mr. Richards thought it was a great idea; he had received a copy of the survey several weeks earlier. However, he felt that the existing survey didn't adequately explore every area he thought it should. "Therefore," said Mr. Richards, "we are revising the survey some-what, and we'll send it out to you when we have it finished."

Mr. Michaelson wanted to speak up about the survey but thought better of it, knowing that confronting the superintendent about the survey changes in front of an audience could be a poor career move. It was, after all, the middle of the school year, and finding a new principal position in another district would be tricky. He let the issue go.

Three weeks later, every principal in the district received the same two surveys. There was one for each teacher and staff member at the campus. This survey consisted of 183 questions. Nearly 45 percent of the questions were about central-office practices and support to the campus. Another 12 percent were about the superintendent's effectiveness as a district leader. Whoever had rewritten the survey used the survey Mr. Michaelson had intended to use and added questions to it.

The second survey sent from the central administration office was for parents, and it was much shorter. At only six questions, the survey could be filled out by most parents in less than five minutes.

The superintendent's e-mail that came with the surveys explained that a short parent survey would suffice because he and the school board ran the charter district, not the parents. Mr. Richards also made it clear in his e-mail that the campus survey results would be used for evaluations of all adminis-tration staff. Furthermore, the survey was not to be completed during school hours.

Mr. Michaelson couldn't believe what he had read in the e-mail. Al-though he was new to the charter school environment, in all his years, he had never seen anything like this. The superintendent closed his e-mail by stating that every employee, regardless of position, was to write the survey outside of the school day. They could not be on the clock when they took it.

When he met with his faculty, Mr. Michaelson explained that the superintendent had directed every campus to use the district survey. It was a long survey, but it could be taken over a period of days if necessary because, as long as the survey taker saved the data, the answers would be preserved.

The principal also informed his teachers that they would have to complete the survey outside the school day; this was a directive from the superintendent. All hourly employees, Mr. Michaelson said, should take the survey while on the clock. Then he sent the survey to the parents for whom he had e-mail addresses.

Four weeks later, the survey results were finished. The superintendent had all the results ready for campus principals, and Mr. Michaelson was eager to see what he could learn about his campus. He wanted to take the results back to his team so they could get to work on creating their mission and vision, as well as focus on core values that he knew the teachers and parents shared.

Principal Michaelson was hoping the survey results would be useful. Right away, he noticed two emerging trends, neither of which he found surprising.

The first trend was that teachers felt that, although they were performing their duties well, they would like further professional development opportunities throughout the year. It was district policy to provide ten days of professional development before school began in August. Central office denied professional development requests for all employees, whether instructional assistant, teacher, or administrator, during the academic year.

The second observation Principal Michaelson made was that his faculty and staff did not find central-office policies supportive, nor did they offer the training and information the campus needed to be successful. Every campus mentioned the absence of ongoing professional development throughout the year.

The other principals corroborated Mike Michaelson's discovery. The survey results were similar across all campuses, and several cited specific examples of top-down management; for example, the central-office finance department had to approve all campus purchases regardless of the amount, and district-level administrators repeatedly requested the same student information from campuses.

Rory Richards was furious with the results of the survey, saying that no one had taken it seriously. In a meeting, he yelled at the central-office administrators for building an inferior product. Then he excoriated the principals for not demanding that their teachers and support personnel tell the truth about central office. Mr. Richards grabbed a handful of papers, tore them into shreds, and stormed out of the room.

They hadn't even seen the parent survey yet, but Principal Michaelson was done.

3. Issue

Principal Michaelson had hoped to use valid survey results for the work he wanted to do with his campus as they built their mission and vision for student achievement. Their core values included honesty and integrity, and Mr. Michaelson knew he could trust his teachers to assess their work and campus needs honestly. However, the central-office administrators revised the survey, making it significantly longer and mostly about themselves and the superintendent.

The superintendent also directed the principals to make campus employees take the survey outside of the school day. Mr. Michaelson defied this directive by allowing his nonexempt employees to take the survey while on the clock.

When the results came back, the superintendent was unprofessional in reviewing the survey answers with his staff. The results, however, showed that the faculty's answers at Best Charter Elementary School closely mirrored those of all the other campuses in the district.

4. Dilemma

The survey that the central-office administration redesigned was an inferior product that likely produced skewed results. However, the results of the survey revealed three important points. First, the teachers were not provided the professional development they needed. Second, central-office procedures consisted of micromanagement and top-down deployment of initiatives and procedures.

And finally, the superintendent refused to accept the results the survey he produced. Instead, he placed blame on others without exploring whether there could be any truth to the statements made.

Principal Michaelson was clearly uncomfortable with the way the survey had been handled, and he also recognized that his philosophy for building the mission, vision, and core values of his school differed significantly from the superintendent's. In addition, he refused to follow one of the superintendent's directives.

As Mr. Michaelson sat in the administrative meeting with the other principals and the central-office staff, he realized that his education philosophy was very different from his boss's.

5. Questions

1. How aligned were Principal Michaelson's intentions for the survey with school leadership standards for professional educational leaders?
2. What problems did the revised surveys create?
3. Was Mr. Michaelson right in defying his superintendent's directive to require nonexempt employees to take the survey while "on the clock"? Why or why not?
4. What should Mr. Michaelson do with the survey results he received?
5. How should Mr. Michaelson handle himself at the meeting with the other administrators and the superintendent? What could his next options be?

---

1. Workroom Whispers

Grade Level: Suburban Elementary School, Grades PK–5
Standard: 1c, Mission, Vision, and Core Values

2. Background

The culture at Valleyview Elementary had always been one of acceptance and support. Located in a diversely populated neighborhood, the school became the center of communication and understanding.

That was largely due to Principal Robin White's approach to working with people. She sought to understand the needs of others before taking care of her own needs. She volunteered her time to help out at local nonprofits, including the thrift store and the food bank. When she drove through the neighborhood, she waved to the parents who were outside, and sometimes she stopped for a visit.

Principal White didn't judge others, and that's what so much of the community appreciated about her. They knew that this principal wouldn't judge their kids, either. They could be accepted for who they are. The parents hoped that all of the teachers were the same way, and for the most part, they were.

Mrs. White hired teachers based on three things: their passion for kids, their ability to teach, and their willingness to accept diversity.

At least 80 percent of the faculty fit this description perfectly; Mrs. White had hired most of them. She had inherited the other 20 percent from a previous principal. These teachers were often negative about many of the new initiatives sent from the district and about the types of children enrolling in the school then; sometimes, this negativity carried over to their colleagues.

The behaviors were most evident when it had been a particularly tiring week and the teachers hung out in the workroom together. Ostensibly, they were there to plan, but often the sessions turned into gripe sessions, and the teachers became harpy-like as they discussed those not present.

Sometimes the discussions centered on the administrative team, including the two assistant principals and Mrs. White.

"That Pollyanna," they'd say of their principal. "She's such a Goody Two-shoes, always helping others. She should take off those rose-colored glasses and see what the world really looks like."

Mrs. White felt that she did have a good idea of what the world was like. Her student population was 30 percent African American, 30 percent Hispanic, and 30 percent white, with the rest Native Americans or Pacific Islanders. The principal tried to hire faculty members who fit that same 30/30/30/10 ratio, and she was pretty close.

In addition, the teachers represented the following categories: single, highly religious, agnostic, young, middle-aged, and older. In short, the faculty was diverse.

Even the two newest teachers, Sara Aimes and Bev Lockhart, represented diversity. They were the first gay teachers Mrs. White had hired—that she knew of.

The principal had been looking forward to the teachers joining the faculty; both women had come from prestigious Ivy League universities, and they were passionate advocates for kids. Mrs. White only discovered that they were gay because she had looked at their social media posts before hiring them.

Their orientation had little to do with their teaching, so the principal recommended them without hesitation.

Ms. Aimes and Ms. Lockhart were equally excited to be teaching at Valleyview with Mrs. White. Their educational philosophies were very similar.

During lunchtime, several of the teachers gathered in the workroom. The negative group sat together as they always did. Nelly Gonzalez sat hunkered over in a chair, scrolling through her phone.

"Well, whaddaya know," she said. "Look at this!" Mrs. Gonzalez passed her mobile phone around to the others at the table.

"Are you kidding me?" said Maureen House.

"OMG, she's lesbo-dyke," said another teacher.

The group fell into using negative and demoralizing descriptions of the two new teachers like buzzards falling on carrion.

They began making fun of the two teachers, then surmised that perhaps Mrs. White was just like them because it takes one to know one. The comments became increasingly degrading, especially about sex. One of the teachers said, "I bet she tries to turn all of her students into little lesbians, too."

Mrs. Gonzalez looked up and froze. "How long have you been standing there?" she asked Ms. Lockhart.

"Long enough to know who my true friends aren't," said Bev Lockhart. She turned on her heels and went directly to Mrs. White's office.

"I'm here to file a complaint," said Ms. Lockhart to her principal, "for sexual harassment."

Mrs. White invited the teacher into her office so they could talk about the situation. The principal advised Ms. Lockhart that she would need to put the complaint in writing and that there would be consequences for any guilty parties. She could not, however, reveal what those were. What she could do was make sure that the harassment never occurred again.

Mrs. White went to the workroom to talk to the teachers who had been so negative.

"That's a load of garbage," said Ms. Gonzalez. "I did not harass that woman. I only called her a lesbo-dyke."

3. Issue

On a campus that says it values diversity and acceptance, several of the teachers have been overheard bullying some of their colleagues. In doing so, they are not modeling the behaviors for which the campus has become known throughout the community.

One of the new teachers who was gay has overheard another teacher calling her and her friend derogatory names. That teacher does not understand how these names are derogatory.

4. Dilemma

The new teacher claims that she is the victim of sexual harassment. She has gone to the principal to seek relief from the name-calling.

The principal took the matter seriously, even asking the teacher to put in writing what she had heard. Then, when the principal went to confront the teachers, the teacher who said some of the ugliest and most harassing statements did not understand how what she said was so wrong.

5. Questions

1. Did Ms. Lockhart have the right to tell the principal that she had been harassed sexually?
2. What should Mrs. White do about Nelly Gonzalez and the other teachers? What, if any, consequences should they receive?

3. The principal goes to address the teachers in the workroom. What's wrong with this idea?
4. Can the principal stop teachers from accessing social media during their lunch period?
5. What help can Mrs. White provide for Ms. Gonzalez, who doesn't understand why her words are inappropriate.

1. Viral Video

Grade Level: Urban Elementary School, Grades PK–5
Standards: 1g, Mission, Vision, and Core Values; 2d, Ethics and Professional Norms

2. Background

John Johnson is a kindergarten teacher at Mandeville Elementary, and Principal Stuart Blackwell was pleased to add Mr. Johnson to the faculty because he could be such a tremendous role model for the kids.

Mr. Johnson is a young black male and the first in his family to earn a college degree and work in a professional field. Although his grades in college weren't the highest, he had many other qualities Mr. Blackwell wanted to promote among his faculty. Mr. Johnson had been active in a variety of campus organizations, including some intramurals and student political affiliations. During his interview, he had told Principal Blackwell about his good fortune in being able to get loans so that he could support himself while attending school full time. It wasn't easy, he had said, but he did it.

Mr. Blackwell thought that kind of determination would inspire students and staff alike, as well as model the school's mission and vision statement: to promote the learning and safety of all students through respect and dignity. Mr. Blackwell recommended that the school board hire Mr. Johnson.

Mr. Johnson's first few months as a teacher went surprisingly well. His class had 40 percent black students, 30 percent Hispanic students, and 30 percent white students. He planned his lessons well in advance and collaborated with the other teachers; not only the students but also the parents really seemed to like him.

In the middle of the fall semester, Mr. Johnson needed time off from work. He explained that he thought he was coming down with something;

perhaps he was tired, but just in case, he wanted to take a Friday off in October.

Mr. Blackwell saw no reason to deny the request—it was made in plenty of time to secure a substitute for the classroom, and Mr. Johnson had the days.

The kindergarten teacher returned to work on Monday, refreshed and ready to go. It seemed that the day off had helped him immensely.

Two weeks, later, however, Mr. Johnson needed another Friday off—and maybe Monday, too. Thinking little of it, Mr. Blackwell approved the request.

Again, Mr. Johnson returned to the classroom, full of energy and ready to teach. Observations revealed that he engaged the kids in learning and had activities mostly ready to go—there was an incident where he couldn't find a set of math manipulative for his students—but for the most part his teaching remained on par.

Within weeks, however, Mr. Johnson was absent again on a Friday. This time, he failed to call in sick. The students assembled in the classroom; after thirty minutes, the instructional assistant reported to the office that the teacher had not yet arrived. What should she do?

Thinking something horrible had happened, Principal Blackwell phoned Mr. Johnson.

Mr. Johnson answered his phone sounding groggy. He could hardly be understood, and it sounded as though he was about to lose his voice. "Who is this, man?" he said.

Mr. Blackwell identified himself and said, "Are you okay? You haven't shown up for work and didn't call. I've been a little worried."

Mr. Johnson assured his principal that he was fine, that he just forgot to call. And he needed Monday off, too. "I'm a little hoarse. I may be getting laryngitis or something."

On Monday, Mr. Blackwell didn't have to wonder about Mr. Johnson. Over the weekend, a video of the kindergarten teacher had begun to make the rounds on social media. The video was more than five minutes in length, and it took place on one of the streets near the school. In fact, the principal recognized the school's roofline in the background.

In the foreground was Mr. Johnson. He stood before a small crowd of people with a megaphone in his hand. To one side waved a Black Lives Matter flag. Nearby, a metal trashcan had been set on fire, and it was burning brightly.

Mr. Johnson held the megaphone up and spoke.

The teacher decried what he called "the system," which he felt was pitted against persons of color. He made negative statements about public education and public housing, as well as city, state, and national government, all of which, in his opinion, serve to control citizens. What they needed is a revolution, and they need it now.

Mr. Johnson peppered his five-minute diatribe with seventy-four uses of profanity, some of it extremely crass and vulgar and none of it appropriate for students' ears. The profanity was mild compared to the rest of the content in the speech.

In addition to attacking public systems, Mr. Johnson accused white people of keeping black and Native Americans down, and he said that, although whites owe other races reparation, all white people should be killed.

He went on to say that the president of the United States should also be murdered and the White House burned to the ground.

The only way to get what he deserves, and for other black people to get what they also deserve, Mr. Johnson yelled into the megaphone, was through violence and upheaval. He needed the crowd's help in taking back what was rightfully theirs from an imperialistic empire insistent on keeping them down as slaves. Together, they had to overturn the evil capitalism that forced them to work as many as forty hours a week.

Principal Blackwell saw the video on Sunday morning when one of the parents stopped him after church to show it to him. "I want my daughter removed from that man's classroom first thing tomorrow morning, or I am going to the school board," she said.

It turned out that she wasn't the only one with a request to remove their child from Mr. Johnson's kindergarten classroom.

By the time Mr. Johnson arrived at the school building Monday morning, almost every parent had called or come by with the same request. As school started, more than half the kindergartners in Mr. Johnson's class were absent. Their parents had kept them home.

3. Issue

Mr. Johnson, a kindergarten teacher at Mandeville Elementary, has been using his sick days to participate in political activities. At first he requested time off in advance, but recently he failed to call in, leaving his classroom without a teacher.

After his most recent absences, a video surfaced of Mr. Johnson. In it, he called on the crowd around him to support overtaking white people and killing them because whites owed reparation to blacks and other minorities. He also called for the murder of the president of the United States.

The video made the social media rounds, and now the parents are requesting that their children be placed in a different teacher's classroom.

4. Dilemma

Mr. Blackwell faces several situations.

Mr. Johnson has incited public disorder by calling for murder. This video was seen by most of the parents, but it also went viral; much of the nation had seen the video by Monday morning. So had the Secret Service.

The parents, who do not realize Mr. Johnson is also absent this Monday, are in a panic trying to get their children moved to another kindergarten teacher's classroom. Also, only half of Mr. Johnson's class came to school; the other half are absent.

The school phones are ringing off the hook with requests for interviews, verbal attacks against the school, and threats against Mr. Blackwell himself for hiring Mr. Johnson in the first place.

On a lesser scale, Mr. Johnson also lied about the use of his sick days.

5. Questions

1. What problem should Mr. Blackwell handle first?
2. How do your recommendations change if you know that Mr. Blackwell is white? What if he is black?
3. What support could Mr. Blackwell request from the school district?
4. What should Mr. Blackwell do about Mr. Johnson?
5. How soon should Mr. Blackwell have confronted Mr. Johnson about the absences?
6. What about Mr. Johnson's right of freedom of speech under the First Amendment?

1. Fifth-Grade Follies

Grade Level: Urban Elementary School, Grades K–5
Standards: 2b, d, e, Ethics and Professional Norms

2. Background

The end-of-the-year talent show at Lincoln Elementary was always a much-anticipated event. The students, teachers, and especially the parents loved the talent show. Rehearsals took place during the last month of school, and although every grade level had at least one entry in the talent show, the fifth-graders were always given preference for most of the slots because they were completing their elementary careers and moving on to middle school.

Ms. Juanita Garcia, the principal, was also looking forward to the show. She felt that her students and teachers deserved a break from instruction, and the talent show was a great opportunity for everyone to come together and have a little fun. This was Ms. Garcia's first year as the principal at Lincoln Elementary.

Traditionally, Miss Redman organized the show, held auditions, and worked with each act so that they performed at their best. She was the show's emcee; she even wore an evening gown to the show.

The other teachers were happy to let Miss Redman take charge of the talent show. It was a lot of work, and it took a lot of time. At this point in the school year, most of the teachers were exhausted and didn't want another responsibility.

Not Miss Redman. She seemed to have endless energy, almost as though she saved it up for this one event. She used her conference period and lunchtime to work with student groups interested in auditioning for the show. She even met after school with students so that everyone who wanted to try out had the opportunity to do so.

She also wanted students to come to her apartment on the weekends to rehearse their songs and performances, but when Principal Garcia heard about that practice, she put a stop to it immediately.

Ms. Garcia met with Miss Redman and said, "I have heard that in the past, you invited students to your home to rehearse."

"Yes, that's true," said Miss Redman.

"You are taking a risk by doing that, jeopardizing your professional licensure and your career. From now on, all rehearsals are to take place at the campus, and I recommend that you have another teacher present as well."

Miss Redman agreed to the changes.

One afternoon, Ms. Garcia stopped by the cafetorium to see how the process was going. She walked in on a group of fifth-grade girls dancing provocatively to a fast-paced rock-and-roll song. After listening to one verse and watching the girls, Ms. Garcia walked over to the sound system and turned it off.

"Give us just a minute, girls," said the principal. "I need to talk to Miss Redman, and she won't be able to hear me with the music playing." Ms. Garcia motioned for Miss Redman to join her in a conversation.

"I know this song. It's extremely inappropriate for this age group of children," said Ms. Garcia. "It's degrading to women because of how the men talk about their girlfriends, it has profanity in it, and it's very suggestive. Please find another song."

"But we use this song every year," said Miss Redman. "The kids love it, and it's easy to dance to."

"That's another thing," said Ms. Garcia. "Those dance moves are equally inappropriate. This is a school talent show, not a burlesque show."

"Are you kidding me?" said Miss Redman. "These dance moves are nothing. You ought to see what the cheerleaders at the middle school are doing."

"We are not a middle school, Miss Redman."

"Well, I've always taught these dance steps and moves. It's never been an issue until now."

Ms. Garcia said, "And I expect it not to be an issue because you will make the necessary changes. I look forward to seeing them in the talent show next week."

By the day of the show, the weather had taken a turn for the worse, and Ms. Garcia developed a cough and began running a fever. She was so ill on the day of the talent show that she had to go home early, but she left everything in the capable hands of her assistant principal, who agreed to take her place as the administrator at the show.

The talent show took place early in the evening. As in the past, Miss Redman showed up in a divine evening gown. She never wore the same dress twice, and this year's dress was shocking. The front and the back plunged to a deep V, seemingly held in place by magic. When she took the stage, Miss Redman had the attention of most of the dads in the audience.

As each group performed, the audience applauded wildly for the children; the children obviously loved the praise. They took bow after bow before relinquishing the stage to the next group.

Finally, the group of fifth-grade girls took their places on the stage, standing still until the music began. The first few bars of the song played on the speaker system. It was the song Ms. Garcia expressly forbade. The girls even danced the same routine the principal had seen the prior week during rehearsals.

The assistant principal wasn't sure what to do. Pull the plug? Close the curtain? Let the group perform? Several parents were videoing the performance with their phones.

When the girls finished their routine, the cafeteria was silent. No one applauded until finally, one parent began polite applause and others joined in. Apparently, none of the adults expected a performance like this.

Neither did Ms. Garcia when she saw the video that had been posted to a social media site later that evening.

3. Issue

Miss Redman clearly defied her principal's directive to change both the song and the dance routine to something more age appropriate.

Not only did she have her students perform the song anyway, but it appears that she did it because the principal was home ill. It seemed like the perfect opportunity to do what she had originally planned.

The performance apparently shocked the parents in the audience as much as it shocked the principal during the rehearsal. The parents didn't know whether to applaud, and even the assistant principal had no idea what to do.

In addition, Miss Redman intentionally wore a revealing dress to an elementary school performance rather than dressing in a more professional manner.

Miss Redman's attire and the dance by the fifth-grade girls were filmed and posted on several social media sites. By the time Ms. Garcia saw the post, there had been hundreds of shares and comments.

4. Dilemma

Miss Redman defied the principal's directive by allowing the original routine to be performed at the talent show. She wore an equally provocative dress to the show; the dress revealed more than it covered.

Surprised parents had apparently never seen this routine before. Their delayed applause suggested that they weren't sure how to respond to the performance. Even the assistant principal had been unprepared for the routine that the fifth-grade girls performed.

With the video on social media sites, the girls' rights may have been violated unless there were photo/video permission slips on file with the school. The other challenge was that there were hundreds of shares and comments, effectively branding the school in a way that it did not want to be.

5. Questions

1. What follow-up should Ms. Garcia have done?
2. How should Ms. Garcia have prepared the assistant principal for supervising the talent show on performance night?
3. What should the assistant principal have done during the performance?
4. What action should Ms. Garcia take in responding to the video of the dance routine posted on social media sites?
5. What consequences should Miss Redman face, if any?

———◈◈◈———

1. Sticks and Stones

Grade Level: Urban Elementary School, Grades PK–5
Standard: 2e, Ethics and Professional Norms

2. Background

Mike Stanford enrolled in Mumsville Elementary in October. He was in the fifth grade, and this was going to be his third placement that year.

The Stanfords scheduled a meeting with Principal Thomas Franklin the week before Mike would actually start classes. He was special, they insisted.

Mr. Franklin welcomed the parents into his office and offered them water or coffee. They both accepted, and Mr. Franklin could tell by the several large folders they brought with them that this might be a much longer meeting than he had expected. Surprisingly, they didn't bring Mike.

They had his birth certificate, and they began with that. Mike, they said, was adopted at the age of four. He had been through several foster homes by that time because the foster parents couldn't handle him or wouldn't let him express himself the way he wanted to.

The Stanfords fostered Mike, and within the year, they knew that they wanted to be his parents forever. In fact, they were certain that Mike had found his forever home, where he would be accepted for who he was. Paul Stanford passed Mike's birth certificate to the principal.

Mr. Franklin looked at it.

"Um, this says Micaela Gibson Stanford. And it indicates that he's a girl."

Paul Stanford affirmed that the information was correct. "He is a girl, or at least that's the sex he was born with. But that's not how he *identifies*."

"Right," said Cooper Stanford. "He really does see himself as a boy. Who better to know that than his two dads?"

"Exactly," said Paul. "Since we've known him, Mike has always acted like a boy. He is more comfortable functioning in a world of maleness, and we'd like to encourage that for as long as Mike wants us to. We left his name 'Micaela' on the birth certificate when we adopted him, just in case he wants to reverse his identify."

"Oh, like that could so happen," laughed Cooper.

Principal Franklin looked from one parent to the other.

"In the meantime, we'd like Mike enrolled as 'Mike' in the school. You know, on the records and such. That way, for now, his identity is consistent. And no one will know that he is physically a female," said Paul.

"Look at his picture," insisted Cooper Stanford. "I think he's the epitome of a young man." He passed the picture to Mr. Franklin.

Mr. Franklin looked at the parents. "Mr. Stanf—, uh Paul. And Cooper. I can't enroll Mike as a male student in our school, and here's why."

The principal carefully explained his position, and the Stanfords listened intently.

"You're the first principal who has been able to explain your reasoning so well," said Paul. "I can see where you are coming from. We just don't want to see him bullied anymore."

Cooper nodded.

"I really do think this is going to be the school where Mike can succeed on his own terms. What do you think, Hon?" asked Paul.

"I couldn't agree more," said Cooper.

The Stanfords agreed with Mr. Franklin's suggestion to bring Mike to school at the end of this week for an orientation. The principal suggested that Mike could visit some of the more important areas of the school, like the library, and end the day meeting with his new teacher.

"Perfect," said the Stanfords.

On Friday afternoon the Stanfords introduced Mike to the principal. Somewhat shyly, Mike stuck out his hand timidly to shake Mr. Franklin's hand. The principal introduced everyone to the counselor, who would be conducting the tour.

Unfortunately, Mike's teacher was absent that afternoon due to illness, but the counselor showed Mike where his classroom would be and assured him that his new teacher would be glad to see him.

In the meantime, the principal called the teacher at home to let her know about the new student she would have in her classroom on Monday. "He's rather special," Mr. Franklin said, and then he explained the situation.

On Monday morning, the teacher was still ill and had a substitute.

Not knowing anyone, the substitute called out the student names to check attendance. "Micaela? Micaela?" The sub looked around the room. No one answered, but everyone in the class starred pointedly at the new kid.

"Are you Micaela?" she asked.

"Mike," mumbled the new student. "Mike. They call me Mike."

At that, the boys in class erupted in laughter and insults.

"A sissy boy named Micaela."

"Do you use the girl's bathroom or the boy's bathroom?"

Even the girls began laughing.

The substitute did the only thing she could think of. She called the principal.

3. Issue

Adoptive parents have brought their son to enroll him in school; this will be the child's third school placement in a year. He had been bullied at the other two schools for identifying as a boy even though his records say he is a girl.

The parents prefer that no one mention that Mike is actually a girl; that includes not using his legal name.

The principal assured the parents that the transition would be a smooth one and no bullying would be tolerated.

4. Dilemma

Mike's teacher was absent when he arrived for orientation and again for his first day of school. A substitute in charge of the classroom called the roll and read Mike's legal name out loud. When the other students in the classroom heard the teacher call him Micaela, they began to laugh and make derogatory remarks. The substitute called for the principal to come to the classroom, and by the time he got there, the students were saying ugly things, and Mike was in tears.

5. Questions

1. What did the principal likely tell the parents about using their child's legal name at school?
2. Was the counselor an appropriate choice to provide the orientation? Why or why not?
3. Was Mr. Franklin right to call the teacher when she was home ill? Why or why not?
4. What should have happened when the teacher's substitute came to work instead of the teacher?
5. What resources can Mr. Franklin involve in the situation?
6. Should Mr. Franklin call Mike's parents or let it go?

1. Because I Said So

Grade Level: Urban Elementary School, Grades PK–5
Standards: 2a, b, Ethics and Professional Norms

2. Background

Principal Bruce Franklin was excited to be the new administrative leader at New Rockford Elementary. The Title I school in a poverty-stricken urban neighborhood was in dire need of new leadership. The school had been looking for a principal who could bring insightful vision and tremendous energy to the campus.

That's exactly what Mr. Franklin intended to do. The new principal wanted to begin his tenure by elevating the standards for all children. Meeting the high expectations set forth by the faculty, he thought, was the only way students would be successful. Mr. Franklin had reviewed the last five years' worth of student performance data from New Rockford Elementary. Over and over again, students came close to performing well on standardized assessments, but they couldn't seem to overcome the final hurdles in passing. As a rule, the students had consistently excellent grades.

Curiously enough, the New Rockford students made mostly As and Bs in their classes; their standardized assessments, however, showed that students performed between the fiftieth and seventieth percentiles—sometimes even lower, in spite of the good grades they had been making.

Mr. Franklin met with his faculty at the beginning of the year. His message was "No child at New Rockford fails." The faculty appreciated their principal's positive attitude. They truly wanted their students to see success in every classroom.

"Your students *will* be successful," said Mr. Franklin. "They have you for their teachers. They simply cannot fail."

The teachers began the year on a positive note. They were excited to teach their students, and they wanted the best for them. The teachers were sure their students could not fail.

A few students seemed to have difficulty with learning, in spite of everyone's positive attitude and high expectations. When the third week of the six-week reporting period came and went, Mr. Franklin was surprised at how many students were in danger of failing.

The principal met with his teachers during their grade-level meetings. With each team, he made it very clear that the students were not to fail. It didn't matter if the students were in 504 plans, special education, gifted and talented classes, or general education. The teachers had to do everything in their power to help the students pass.

"We're working very hard in class with the students," several of the teachers pointed out. "They are getting there."

A few of the teachers made excuses for their students, saying, "You know they come from poor environments," or "The parents do their job raising their children. It's not fair that we have to be the parents, too."

"None of that matters," said Mr. Franklin. "The students have to pass."

When the grading period concluded, Mr. Franklin reviewed student grades with the teachers. As he chaired each grade-level meeting, he gave every teacher a list of the students who had failed at least one class. Some teachers had as many as a dozen students on their lists.

"This is unacceptable," said Mr. Franklin. "One of the ways we measure success at this campus is by the percentage of students who pass all of their classes. Not all students are passing their classes, and this is not okay."

After the second grading period came and went, Mr. Franklin handed out the lists of failing students again. Many of the teachers had much shorter lists than before. "Why do we still have failing students?" asked Mr. Franklin. He pounded his fist on the table. "I said this is not okay. I want to see everyone passing. If a student is in danger of failing, you have to try every means possible to get him or her to pass, period!"

Again, the teachers went back to their classrooms. Some of the teachers began offering tutorials and found other creative ways to reteach concepts to the students who had failed. Not all of the teachers invested this much effort into helping students pass, so when the third grading period ended, Mr. Franklin met individually with each teacher and brought the list of students who were failing at least one class.

The office staff could hear the principal yelling and screaming behind the closed door of his office, and several teachers left the meetings in tears.

When the fourth grading period ended, Mr. Franklin was all smiles at the grade-level meetings with his teachers. He tossed the grade record sheets on the table in front of the teachers. "Look at this," he said. "You did it! One hundred percent of our students are passing their classes."

Sure enough, the grade sheets showed that there wasn't a failing grade anywhere. Upon closer examination of the grades, however, a keen observer would have noticed that some of the students who had been consistently failing during the first three grading periods were now passing—barely—with a 70. In fact, students of the teachers who had had to meet with Mr. Franklin in his office after the last grading period all had 70s, in every subject.

"You see," said Mr. Franklin, "I knew all along it was possible. Not one of our students at New Rockford Elementary is failing. Outstanding work!"

Soon the students participated in their annual achievement tests, the tests that determined their learning progress, the effectiveness of the teachers' instruction, and how well the campus performed as a whole compared to campuses of similar demographics across the state.

Mr. Franklin was devastated when he got his campus scores back. Not only had many of his students failed the assessment in all subject areas, but the scores this year were considerably lower than in past years. Nearly half of the students at New Rockford Elementary failed at least one portion of the state assessment. Another quarter of them failed all parts of the state assessment.

"How could this be?" Mr. Franklin wondered.

He wasn't the only one curious about the outcome of the state assessment. Irate parents already wanted to schedule appointments with him. They were demanding to know why their child had been passing their classes all year long, only to find out that they not only failed the high-stakes state assessment but also, in many instances, regressed in learning from the previous year.

3. Issue

The principal's attitude that no student could fail at his school was a noble one, especially if his teachers worked tirelessly with every student to help him or her overcome any learning challenges.

However, Mr. Franklin became increasingly insistent that children were not allowed to fail. He wanted to see passing grades. He measured his campus success by how many students were passing their subjects, and he berated teachers, both publicly and privately, for not meeting the standard he set for New Rockford Elementary.

Mr. Franklin was satisfied when all of the students finally passed their subjects, even if it meant that they had all 70s, but this happiness was short-lived when the high-stakes assessment results became public.

Half of the students failed, showing a disconnect somewhere. Was the disconnect in the inflated grades? Could teachers have made up grades or graded on a curve so that students would pass—and Mr. Franklin would stop complaining?

4. Dilemma

Now that the parents of students at New Rockford Elementary have seen their child's assessment results, they are shocked. They are in disbelief that their children did not pass the assessments, especially because they had passed all of their subjects—the report cards said so.

Failing the state assessment meant repeating a grade level. In this case, nearly 50 percent of the students would have to repeat the grade that they were in. This unexpected turn of events created a change in the staffing pattern for the following year.

It also gave the parents a valid argument for school choice. Why would they want their children at a school where they were going to fail the one assessment that matters the most? Many of the parents now want to meet with the superintendent about transferring their children to another school in the district.

5. Questions

1. What should Mr. Franklin have said to be sure that his teachers understood what he meant when he said "No child at New Rockford fails"?

2. On a scale of 1 to10, with 10 being the highest, what is the likelihood of teachers making up grades? Justify your response.
3. How should Mr. Franklin have handled the grade-level meetings differently?
4. What are some steps a principal should take to ensure that the grades are not inflated or falsified?
5. Should parents be allowed to go to a school of choice instead of attending New Rockford Elementary next year?

—※※※—

1. Not in My School

Grade Level: Rural Elementary School, Grades K–5
Standards: 1c, Mission, Vision, and Core Values; 2f, Ethics and Professional Norms; 8h, Meaningful Engagement of Families and Community

2. Background

Jenny Baumeister was the kind of principal who loved people.

"School is a people business," she'd tell her faculty. "First and foremost, we have to make sure that people—the kids, their parents, and the community—know that they matter to us. There is no greater thing we can do than to ensure that we meet the needs of our community and their children."

Ms. Baumeister backed her words up with actions. Every year, she led her faculty in community outreach activities. Several times a year, not just at Thanksgiving, the campus held canned-food drives. In the winter, the campus collected coats and blankets to share with those in the community needing warm clothing and bedding.

The campus hosted a fall festival and a spring fling as opportunities for parents to bring their children to a safe place for good old-fashioned family fun. Kids played games at various stations, and the faculty and staff oversaw the fun. There was even a dunking booth—and both the assistant principal and the principal took their turns sitting above the tank of water.

The teachers took turns supervising the computer lab for students after school and on Saturday mornings when parents couldn't always get to school to pick up their children. Some parents had to work or run errands on Saturdays. The school was there for the community, and the kids were supervised in an educational environment. Even other faculty members, like the librarian, volunteered to come in and help.

Ms. Baumeister intended the school to not only be the crossroads of the community but also set the example for model behavior—on campus and beyond. She expected her teachers to conduct themselves professionally on campus and to extend that same professionalism to after-hours activities.

By making sure her faculty was always professional, she could hold them up as examples to the parents. Her teachers and staff would set the standard, she felt. She had seen small successes firsthand, and she knew more would follow. Most parents began to look up to the teachers, and they respected them greatly.

Ms. Baumeister also made sure her teachers and staff were taken care of. When Ms. Coleman was diagnosed with breast cancer, the principal organized meals for the stricken teacher and her family. When teacher Lucas Chavarria and his wife decided to adopt a child, Ms. Baumeister opened a funding site to help the young married couple with adoption expenses.

No principal was there more for her staff than Ms. Baumeister. She was invited to share in their celebrations and losses, which she did. The principal had worked hard to create a loving and supporting family of teachers and staff.

Ms. Baumeister also loved organization and structure, which she felt helped to fine-tune the school processes. Drop-off times in the morning were established according to parent need rather than teacher convenience. Recess duty was scheduled to provide more than adequate coverage for the supervision of children at play.

Even the parent pick-up times and traffic patterns had been carefully studied and designed to ensure that parents could easily and safely pick up their children after school.

Those children who did not ride the bus or walk home—or stay for one of the after-school activities—stood in lines on the front lawn of the school to wait for their parents to pick them up. Each grade, from PK to 5, stood in its respective group. As parents drove slowly past the grade-level lines, they picked up their children and drove on.

Many of the teachers and Ms. Baumeister stood in the parking lot to supervise the children during pick-up times. Ms. Baumeister often talked to the parents in their cars as they drove along the line. It didn't matter if the weather was freezing, too hot, or rainy; the principal and teachers stood with their students until the last student had been collected. Afternoon duty lasted no more than ten to twelve minutes. During that time, they saw 250 students get picked up.

On one particularly warm day, a shiny object in one of the cars caught Ms. Baumeister's eyes. Surely the principal wasn't seeing what she initially thought it was. She looked again.

Sure enough, the shiny object between the legs of the man driving the car was a beer can. He was in line to pick up his second- and fourth-graders, plus a couple of their friends.

Ms. Baumeister told the parent that alcohol was not permitted on campus and that having an open container of alcohol prevented him from picking up the children.

"What do you want me to do?" he asked.

"You can let your friend drive, if she hasn't been drinking." Ms. Baumeister pointed to the woman sitting in the seat next to the man. "Or I will have to ask you to pull over until someone who has not been drinking can drive your car home for you. I cannot let you pick up children and drive them anywhere."

"You have a lot of nerve," said the parent. "I have to be at work in twenty minutes, and you're gonna make me late," he said.

"No, you are making yourself late," said Ms. Baumeister. "You shouldn't drink and drive."

The man laughed. "Really? Are you going to go there? What do you think your librarian does?"

"Excuse me?" asked Ms. Baumeister.

"Sure, that woman drinks and drives. I seen her taking a nip while at the wheel. She lives in the same apartment complex as me and my kids."

"You don't know that," said Ms. Baumeister. "You can't know that."

"Whatever," said the parent. "But I bet she even drinks while on the job."

With that, he got out of his car, switching places with his girlfriend. The children got in the car, and she drove off.

Ella Strand, the school librarian, was no alcoholic—of that Ms. Baumeister was certain. But was she drinking at work?

3. Issue

Ms. Baumeister has taken a two-pronged approach to structuring her school. On the one hand, she has created an environment where community needs determine campus direction and support. In the few years she has been principal at the school, Ms. Baumeister has developed a compassionate faculty attuned to supporting the parents and their community. As a result, everyone looks to the school for more than education. It is the heartbeat of the community.

On the other hand, Ms. Baumeister has set high standards for her faculty, and she expects every faculty and staff member to be the role model for others. The teachers are both professional and courteous.

A parent has shown up to pick up his two children after school. He has an open container of alcohol between his legs.

When confronted about the beer, he informs Ms. Baumeister that her librarian also drinks and drives and probably drinks while at work.

4. Dilemma

Ms. Baumeister has been confronted with accusatory information. When she stopped one of the parents at the after-school pick-up area for drinking and driving, he pointed out that the principal had a double standard—one for the community and one for her employees.

Although Ms. Baumeister had established high expectations of her faculty and staff, the parent revealed that the school librarian, Mrs. Ella Strand, had been seen drinking and driving in the community. The parent further raised the suspicion that the librarian has been drinking secretly at work.

5. Questions

1. What happens in schools can dramatically shape how students come to see the world. How should administrators want students to see the world?
2. How can this be tied to a school's mission?
3. Was Ms. Baumeister right to request that the parent find another driver because he had an open container in his vehicle?
4. What do you recommend the principal do if the parent refuses to comply with her request to change drivers? As part of a small, tight-knit community, should she call the parent's employer because he was on the way to work?
5. What steps, if any, should the principal take in regard to the accusation about the librarian?
6. What, if anything, should the principal do if she learns that the parent's accusations are false?
7. What, if anything, should the principal do if she learns that the parent's accusations are true?

Chapter Two

Instructional Leadership and School Improvement

1. Flu Epidemic

Grade Level: Urban Elementary School, Grades PK–5
Standards: 10h, i, School Improvement

2. Background

The school nurse paused by the coffee pot in the workroom to ask Principal Larry Gould if he had had his flu vaccine yet.

"Aw, Tina," he said, "You know I hate those things. Why should I inject myself with a virus I don't want?"

"Mr. Gould, you know my answer to that. You build up immunities quicker so that if you do catch the flu, you won't have it so bad," said Tina Black, the nurse.

Mr. Gould was not the only one at Brook Elementary who refused to get a flu shot. Many of the teachers felt the same way. They'd rather take their chances than get vaccinated.

They got that opportunity during the worst flu season in the last twenty years.

At first, only a couple of the teachers became ill.

Principal Gould didn't think anything of it. Illness happens, and it usually takes only a few days before everyone is back on their feet again.

However, his registrar came down with the flu, and his secretary began showing signs of the virus. She looked as though she had been crying, and she was constantly blowing her nose.

"For the love of Mike," said Principal Gould. "Go see Tina about that. And wipe everything down with disinfectant, would you?"

The attendance numbers at Brook Elementary began to dip dangerously low. They held at 92 percent for a week, then dropped to 90 percent the week after that, and by the third week of the flu epidemic, they had dropped to 78 percent. The faculty and staff numbers nearly matched the students'.

During that third week, Mr. Gould took to the hallways with spray cans of disinfectant. He sprayed everywhere he could think of, even walking through classrooms and spraying them as well.

Students who weren't coughing because of the flu began to cough because of the disinfectant spray, so Mr. Gould decided to wait until after school to continue his war against the virus. Then he resumed his attack with a vengeance.

The next morning, Janie Little's dad was waiting for the principal. There was no one else in the office because the registrar and the secretary were out with the flu.

"My Janie is home sick," said Mr. Little. "I'd like to know what you intend to do about it."

"I'm not a doctor; I'm a principal," said Mr. Gould.

"Exactly," said Mr. Little. "And because you are the principal I expect you to know better. How could you do such a thing?"

"What are you talking about?" said Mr. Gould.

"Janie had to go to the emergency room last night," said her father. "She has asthma, and she nearly quit breathing. Your stupid disinfectant spray triggered her reaction. She could have died."

Mr. Gould was taken aback. He looked genuinely concerned.

"I'm so sorry," he said. "I had no idea. How is she now?"

Mr. Little said that Janie was home resting comfortably, but that was the problem.

Mr. Gould knitted his eyebrows together in a question mark. "How so? What is the problem?"

"Janie has had perfect attendance right here in this school ever single year. This is her fifth-grade year, and she's halfway through that. No absences. Not ever. Until today. And it's your fault."

"My fault?" said Mr. Gould.

"Yeah," said Mr. Little. Then he pushed the principal, just a little.

Mr. Gould reached out toward him in an effort to catch himself, but Mr. Little saw the movement as retaliation; he jerked his arm back, ready to strike. Oddly, his mobile phone was in his hand.

"Whoa, whoa," said Mr. Gould. "I was falling. Let's not get upset here and do something we'll regret."

"I already regret sending my daughter to this school," said Mr. Little. "Perfect attendance, and it's gone in a flash, just like that." And he snapped his fingers for emphasis.

The principal asked Mr. Little to sit down with him and talk it out.

"What is it you really want?" asked Mr. Gould.

"I want you to mark my daughter present for today. She'll be back at school tomorrow. Her perfect attendance will continue, with no gaps."

Mr. Gould said he couldn't do that.

"You have to do that Mr. Gould. You caused problems when you sprayed the school yesterday with the kids present. I've got video of you trying to rush me just now. If you don't mark my daughter present, I'm sure this little video will go viral."

"Get out," said Mr. Gould. He sat back down in his chair and sneezed.

3. Issue

A particularly bad strain of influenza has taken a hold of the faculty, the staff, and the students at Brook Elementary. Mr. Gould has taken matters into his own hands by singlehandedly trying to disinfect the school while the students were still present. Parents do not want their children to miss school.

The attempt triggered an asthma attack in one of the children, and she had to stay home the next day, marring her perfect attendance record.

4. Dilemma

The absent student's father has shown up at Brook Elementary, demanding that the principal mark the child present so that she will have perfect attendance for her fifth and final year of elementary school. He is ready to blackmail the principal if he doesn't comply.

5. Questions

1. What should Mr. Gould have done as soon as he noticed people were getting sick with the flu?
2. What was the problem with spraying disinfectant in the hallways and classrooms to ward off further infection?
3. Because no other office staff were present during the incident with Mr. Gould and Mr. Little, who could the principal have asked to come to the office? Why would that have been a good thing to do?
4. Should Mr. Gould mark Janie present? Why or why not?
5. What further action should the principal take? Why?

1. Data Matters

Grade Level: Rural Elementary School, Grades 3–5
Standards: 4f, g, Curriculum, Instruction, and Assessment

2. Background

Mr. Zabek is in his second year as the principal of Wrenfield Elementary. His first year on the campus had been a turbulent one. Many of the teachers on his staff told him that they have seen principals come and go, but—regardless of what he tries to do—they'll still be at Wrenfield when he moves on. The sit-and-wait-it-out approach made changing instructional practices difficult, and yet that's what Mr. Zabek had been hired to do.

Historically, the school's state assessment scores teetered back and forth between what the veteran teachers called "okay" and "oops." In some years, at least 75 percent of the students passed the assessments; in others, the campus fell to 65 percent passing. Each time the campus was in danger of losing accreditation, the teachers worked hard enough to pull the scores back up.

The teachers did not implement curriculum-based assessments (CBAs) until Mr. Zabek arrived last year. Before the year started, he worked with a select group of teachers to write the assessments. The campus purchased a software program to facilitate the CBA scoring and data analysis. Scores reached 82 percent passing—a first for Wrenfield Elementary.

The campus is made up of two factions of teachers. The first is a small number of veteran teachers who have managed to stay on the campus in spite of past poor leadership. Most of the veteran teachers have twelve to fifteen years of teaching experience, all earned at Wrenfield.

The second group consists of teachers who are new or nearly new to the teaching profession and those who are new to the campus and district. The trend in the last ten years has been for 90 percent of this teacher group to leave Wrenfield Elementary after two years. Approximately half of them find other teaching jobs within the district, and the other half leave the area completely.

Mrs. Albertson is the lead teacher in fifth grade. She's taught at Wrenfield Elementary for fourteen years. During that time, she worked her way up from rookie teacher right out of college to seasoned veteran. This year, as in the past five years, Mrs. Albertson has elected to teach the top students in the grade level. She feels that she has earned this right. Mr. Zabek asked Mrs.

Albertson to assist the other teachers in the grade level. She refused, saying that holding teachers' hands was not her responsibility. She wanted only to work with students.

Mr. Barrera has been at Wrenfield Elementary for five years. Although his first year was difficult, he has since become an effective teacher, and the students like him. Mr. Barrera spent considerable time during his first year of teaching trying to understand the curriculum and learning how to interpret data. He was never assigned a mentor so he had to figure things out on his own. Since then, he's thought that all new teachers should "learn the ropes" on their own. Mr. Barrera teaches the second-highest group of students.

Mrs. Cody has begun her second year of teaching at Wrenfield Elementary. She still struggles with the basics of lesson planning. Her biggest difficulty is coming up with enough activities for her students. Discipline management is also a challenge. Like Mr. Barrera, she had to figure out on her own what to teach and how to teach it. This year, Mrs. Cody is teaching the second-lowest group. She's told Mrs. Albertson that she's hoping she'll get a "better group of students" someday.

Mrs. Davis is the new teacher on the fifth-grade team. This is her first year at Wrenfield Elementary, and it's also her first year teaching elementary school. She has twelve years of teaching experience at the middle school and high school levels in other districts, but she wanted to teach at the elementary level before going into school administration. She, too, has had difficulty figuring out the scope and sequence of the curriculum.

Mrs. Davis has repeatedly requested assistance; Mr. Zabek told her to go to Mrs. Albertson for assistance. When she did, Mrs. Albertson told her that she didn't help teachers, especially new ones. Mrs. Davis has been assigned the lowest-performing student group, which consists of all the 504-plan and special-education students.

Mr. Zabek decided to continue the CBA implementation. This past summer, he held another weeklong CBA writing camp, and he invited all the most experienced teachers to participate. The goal was to review the assessment alignment based on the data collected over the year and revise the CBAs where necessary. Mrs. Albertson was able to finish her work in four and a half days, so after lunch on the last day she went home early.

When the school year started, Mrs. Albertson, Mr. Barrera, and Mrs. Cody knew about the CBAs. They also had a pretty good idea when they would be given. No one told Mrs. Davis about the assessments, though, until the Friday morning they were to be administered.

"Oh by the way, Mrs. Davis," said Mrs. Albertson, "these are your CBAs. I printed them for you this time, but you'll have to do it from here on out. These CBAs have to be done today and scanned before you go home."

Mrs. Davis tried to explain that she already had her lesson plans in place; both Mr. Zabek and Mrs. Albertson approved them the prior week.

"Plans change," said Mrs. Albertson.

Mrs. Davis administered the CBA to her students, explaining that she, too, was caught off guard by this but had every confidence in her students. She was worried that her students were poorly prepared for the assessment.

She was right. When she scanned the last sets of CBAs late that afternoon, she pulled the data. Her class scored 52 percent passing.

Accordingly, Mrs. Davis spent the weekend revising her lesson plans for the following week so she could help students with areas in which they were having difficulty. Each day, she would reteach the objectives during the warm-up and then work with students during their facilitated work and independent practice. They had two weeks until the next CBA.

Monday morning, she told Mrs. Albertson of her plan.

"Oh, we don't do it that way," said Mrs. Albertson. "Just assign the CBA for homework. Have the kids make test corrections and bring them back sometime during the week."

Mrs. Davis said, "Okay." She had no intention of doing that. She was going to implement her plan.

When the second CBAs were scored, Mrs. Davis was still not pleased with the results, although her students had improved. The class had a 57 percent passing rate.

3. Issue

Mr. Zabek reviewed Mrs. Davis's scores. To help her learn the "Wrenfield Way" of instruction and assessment, he arranged to cover class for Mrs. Davis so she could observe Mrs. Albertson's class for half a day. He had done this last year for Mr. Barrera and Mrs. Cody, and their scores had improved.

Mrs. Davis was less than eager to leave her students with a substitute during a CBA, but she did want to learn how to help her students with theirs. She observed Mrs. Albertson in the classroom.

While administering the CBA, Mrs. Albertson went around the room, conversing softly with each student. She helped them read the questions and the answers on the test, and she did on-the-spot reteaching if students didn't understand what a question was asking.

"It's a learning experience," she told Mrs. Davis.

"Yes, it is," Mrs. Davis agreed.

For the third CBA, Mrs. Davis saw the test in advance. It was not aligned with the curriculum; the test contained several questions from objectives that, according to the scope and sequence, would not be taught until the following six weeks. She rewrote the assessment, making sure it was aligned with what was currently being taught. Then she shared it with the teachers on the team.

Curious, Mrs. Davis pulled the scores for her class and the others:

Mrs. Davis: 72 percent passing
Mrs. Cody: 61 percent passing
Mr. Barrera: 64 percent passing
Mrs. Albertson: 75 percent passing

During the faculty meeting, Mr. Zabek publicly recognized Mrs. Albertson for taking the initiative to realign the CBA.

She took credit for the work while Mrs. Davis fumed.

4. Dilemma

Mr. Zabek's teachers are undermining his efforts to bring curriculum, instruction, and assessment together, but he is unaware of who is doing it. He has allowed the veteran teachers to control curriculum, instruction, and assessment procedures. In doing so, they have taken convenient shortcuts.

Newer teachers have not wanted to rock the boat, so they have said nothing. They found it far easier to say nothing rather than go against the veteran teachers.

Mrs. Davis wants to meet privately with Mr. Zabek. So does Mrs. Albertson.

5. Questions

1. What should Mr. Zabek tell his teachers to look for in last year's CBA data when they are aligning the tests?
2. Which teacher should Mr. Zabek listen to first? Does the order matter?
3. Should Mr. Zabek be alone in the meetings with the teachers? Why or why not?
4. What should Mr. Zabek's next steps be when he learns what happened? Consider how he might address curriculum and instruction, scheduling, professional development, and data analysis.
5. How could Mr. Zabek lead the teachers in improving curriculum, instruction, and assessment at his campus?

———⌘———

1. Story Time

Grade Level: Suburban Elementary School, Grades PK–5
Standards: 4b, d, Curriculum, Instruction, and Assessment

2. Background

The Crawley School District was well-known in academic circles for its outstanding educational program. The district had a large curriculum department that regularly revised and updated their materials, from the scope and sequence for each grade level to the resources for teachers in the classroom.

The district was so advanced in this area that many hopeful teaching candidates wanted to work in Crawley because of the tremendous training and professional development they received. Other districts knew that a teacher who was fortunate enough to get practicum experience in Crawley would be a good hire for their district. Teachers who left Crawley to go to other districts were also hired on the spot.

Crawley set the standard for their professional development in curriculum and instruction. Teachers understood why and how the materials for each unit had been selected and could also articulate what made them outstanding choices for students to use in the classroom.

Even the principals were provided with a strong foundation from the curriculum department so there would be no second-guessing and no wasting money on unnecessary resources. Everything about instruction was intentional in Crawley.

That's why principal Imelda Wise was so surprised when one of the teachers came to her to ask for some supplementary materials for a lesson.

"I'd like to buy a few readers for my classroom library," said Milly Flynn, the second-grade teacher.

"We have an extensive library," said the principal.

"Yes, Mrs. Wise, I know," said Miss Flynn, "but I'd like to supplement— not supplant—the work the district has done and have some additional reading materials in the classroom. I can buy them on sale at the bookstore if I can be reimbursed."

"No," said Mrs. Wise. "We'll do this the right way and get a purchase order. How much do you think you'll need?"

"A hundred dollars will allow me to pick up four to six books," said Miss Flynn. "Is that okay?"

Mrs. Wise said it was and reminded Miss Flynn to bring back her receipt along with the purchase order.

The following week, Miss Flynn turned in everything for her purchases, and the principal didn't think of it again. Books in a classroom are always a great addition.

At least, that's what Mrs. Wise had always thought, until she saw a parent comment on the school's social media page: "Stopped by my daughter's class today. Why are our kids reading smut and trash?"

"That couldn't be," thought Mrs. Wise. The district vetted the curriculum and the materials thoroughly. She was just about to put the issue out of her mind when she thought better of it. Mrs. Wise scrolled down to look at more of the comments. Apparently the incident had taken place in Miss Flynn's room.

The parents wanted to rally together to protest at the next school board meeting.

The principal asked her secretary to get the phone numbers of the parents who were protesting the books. She wanted to talk to them before they went to the school board. She also wanted to talk to Miss Flynn.

"Please bring the books to the office with you," Mrs. Wise told Miss Flynn when she asked to meet with her.

Miss Flynn did as she asked.

Mrs. Wise laid out the five purchased books across her desk. She looked at the book covers and at Miss Flynn.

"Can you tell me why you chose these books to supplement the curriculum?"

"Sure," said Miss Flynn. "We're studying multicultural and diverse communities. I thought it would be a good idea to include literature on the LGBTQIA community as well."

"The . . .?"

"Lesbian, Gay, Bisexual, Transsexual, Queer, Intersex, Asexual community. They are highly underrepresented, you know. It's a much larger population than many people might believe. So many people are afraid to speak out about it."

"It appears that many people *are* afraid that you've been speaking out about it," said Mrs. Wise. "Have you seen the parents' posts on our schools' social-media site?"

"Oh, sure," said Miss Flynn, "and they'll get over it when they see that it's really no biggie."

"No biggie?" said Mrs. Wise. "You do realize that we are talking about second-graders here?"

"Well, of course," said Miss Flynn. She went on to explain that she often and quite openly discussed her own sexual identity in front of her students. She had told the students that she didn't have a boyfriend; she had a girlfriend, and what could possibly be wrong with that?

3. Issue

In a district where all the curriculum materials are chosen carefully for consistent implementation district-wide, Principal Wise has permitted one of her teachers to purchase supplemental reading materials for her second-grade classroom. These purchases are books about having LGBTQIA parents and gender identity. One of the books is considered nonfiction, and it describes the various relationships between people, including sexual ones. The other four books are fictional stories whose characters are LGBTQIA themselves or have parents who are.

4. Dilemma

Some of the parents have seen the books, and instead of coming to talk to the principal, they are mounting a protest to be held at the next school board meeting. The principal found out about the incident only through social media. When she asked the teacher about the situation, the teacher assured her that she had revealed her own sexual preferences to her second-graders.

5. Questions

1. Should Mrs. Wise have allowed the purchase of the supplemental materials? What could she have done to control the books being purchased?
2. Do you recommend that Mrs. Wise speak to the parents individually or as a group? Why?
3. What should Mrs. Wise do with the supplemental books?
4. If you were Mrs. Wise, what would you tell Miss Flynn?
5. Should disciplinary action be taken?

1. More Than a Day on a Calendar

Grade Level: Suburban Elementary School, Grades PK–5
Standards: 4b, d, Curriculum, Instruction, and Assessment

2. Background

The one thing Principal Valerie Leon did well was plan. By the time the beginning of school rolled around, she had already outlined every important event in the school year. These dates were announced on the school calendar, which she printed for the teachers and also put on the school website.

Principal Leon always put together such a great schedule for the year that several of the other elementary schools in the system waited until she posted her calendar and then copied it, adapting it slightly for their own campuses.

One of the many things her faculty loved about Principal Leon was her ability to find reasons to celebrate just about anything. She included those celebrations on the calendar, too. Some of them were obvious, like A-B

Honor Roll assemblies, reading and math awards, perfect attendance, and so on. Then there were the special celebrations.

The celebrations everyone looked forward to the most were the culturally diverse days on the calendar. Mrs. Leon made sure that her campus celebrated Women's Equality Day in August, Diez y Seis de Septiembre during Hispanic Heritage Month in September, National Coming Out Day in October, Eid Milad al-Nabi (Prophet Muhammad's birthday) in November, and the International Human Rights Day in December.

Then there was Martin Luther King Day in January, Black History Month in February, International Women's Day in March, Autism Awareness in April, and Asian American and Pacific Islander Heritage Month in May.

For many of these culturally diverse events, the children put on a performance for their classmates and parents. There was dancing, singing, and food. The food had been carefully selected from each holiday's country of origin, and everyone was invited to sample delicious morsels from around the world.

The teachers and the students enjoyed the diversions brought by the cultural-diversity dates on the calendar, but they didn't always understand why they were celebrating them.

The demographics of Crestview Elementary, where Mrs. Leon was principal, were 82 percent white, 12 percent black, and 6 percent Hispanic students. There were no Asian American or Pacific Islander students at Crestview. Two years earlier, they had had a student who they thought might have been LGBTQIA, but he completed his elementary education and moved on. Crestview had a couple of special-needs kids, including several who were autistic.

Mrs. Leon's goal, however, was to create the most diversified calendar she could produce. Each year she tweaked the events, making them even better than in the previous year. She omitted activities for Christian and Jewish holidays and outdated white-person holidays.

That meant ignoring Christmas, Easter, Hanukkah, Yom Kippur, and Rosh Hashanah. Principal Leon viewed these holidays as outdated observances and religious interference in her school. After all, wasn't there supposed to be a separation of church and state in the public schools? Mrs. Leon knew the answer to that, and she intended to uphold the First Amendment by keeping it that way.

When the teachers asked to hold a door-decorating contest for Christmas, Mrs. Leon said no. When the kindergarten and pre-kindergarten teachers wanted to hold an Easter egg hunt, Mrs. Leon said no. The same thing happened with Jewish holidays. The answer was no.

In October, Mrs. Leon insisted that the third-grade teachers take down the Christopher Columbus displays that the students had worked on. Even traditional rhymes like "In 1492, Christopher Columbus sailed the ocean blue" had to be removed.

Mrs. Leon's logic told her that Columbus's questionable motives for finding a trade route and unacceptable treatment of the natives he discovered were grounds enough to remove the explorer from the history lessons. Columbus was nothing more than a greedy white male who used others—people not at all like him—for personal gain.

It was much more important to celebrate National Coming Out Month, Mrs. Leon told her faculty. Encouraging a child to embrace the person he or she is destined to be is a morally superior decision.

Even Thanksgiving was not going to be recognized.

"It's a white man's holiday in which he used Native Americans. Absolutely not," said Mrs. Leon.

Unfortunately, parents didn't agree with the principal any more than teachers did. During the year, when parents came to the school to drop off or pick up their children, they asked the teachers, "What about decorating for Halloween. Do you need help with creating themes to go with it? Or Thanksgiving?" and "Where are the decorations for Christmas?"

The teachers explained their situation. The principal had already identified other holidays to celebrate. Halloween, Christmas, Yom Kippur, and even Valentine's Day had not made the calendar list this year.

"Why don't you post about this on social media?" asked the parents.

"We can't. Our acceptable-use policy says we'll get fired if we do."

That didn't stop a few determined parents. When everyone sat down that night to watch the local evening news at home, the lead story was "Local School Grinch Shuts Down Christmas." The story, several minutes long, included interviews from the parents and video shots of the halls at Crestview Elementary, with only rainbow-themed student work on the walls.

The next morning at the school, Mrs. Leon pushed her way past a group of irate parents, intent on getting to her office without having to talk to any of them.

As she pulled off her gloves and coat, she listened to the first message on her desk phone.

The superintendent wanted to see her in his office immediately.

3. Issue

Principal Valerie Leon selected celebratory holidays for her campus that represented popular culture and thinking. By celebrating unusual holidays from around the world, the principal felt as though she was providing students with priceless experiences based on diversity and multiculturalism.

Unfortunately, the celebrations Principal Leon placed on the calendar did not match the demographics of her campus, student body, or teaching staff.

She also didn't include any of the teachers or the parents in the planning, and now she has alienated them.

4. Dilemma

Principal Leon handpicked the holidays that her campus would be celebrating. The teachers were disappointed that traditional favorites had been excluded. Parents who learned that some of their holidays had been ignored threatened to go to the superintendent about the issue. Within twenty-four hours, the issue was on the news, and the superintendent wanted to see her in his office.

5. Questions

1. How should school and district policy be developed? What should the aim be?
2. Was it appropriate to include the holidays indicated? Why or why not?
3. Was it appropriate to exclude the holidays indicated? Why or why not?
4. Is Mrs. Leon's interpretation of the First Amendment accurate? What about her rationale for which holidays to include?
5. Should the teachers have posted their thoughts about the holiday bans on social media? Why or why not?
6. What do you think the superintendent will tell the Mrs. Leon?
7. Make recommendations for celebrating certain holidays and excluding others at the Crestview Elementary campus.

1. Someone Like Me

Grade Level: Urban Elementary School, Grades PK–5
Standards: 4a, Curriculum, Instruction, and Assessment; 5d, Community of Care and Support for Students

2. Background

It was midmorning, and one of the fifth-grade classes at Spartan Elementary had just placed their literature books on their desks. They had just started reading time.

"Turn to page 282, please," said their teacher.

One hand went up immediately.

"Ain't you tired of teaching about them dead white guys yet?" Maxwell Black asked his English teacher, Mrs. Owens.

Mrs. Owens bristled like a cat that had just had water thrown on it.

"And what exactly is the problem with *those* 'dead white guys,' as you call them, Mr. Black?" she asked.

"Well, for one, they're all white. And they're all dead," said Maxwell. The class snickered and laughed, but when the laughter died down, another student spoke up. It was Vishna Gupta.

"He has a point. We never read anything by writers of color. You know, someone like me," said Vishna.

"Or me," said Carlos.

"Or someone like me," said Maxwell. "And that's my point. It's like only white guys matter, ever."

"Well that's because . . ." Mrs. Owens never got out another word.

Suddenly, the class began chanting, "Black Lives Matter! Black Lives Matter!"

Mrs. Owens tried to quiet her students but couldn't get them to settle back into their chairs. The next thing she knew, several of the students were standing on top of their desks, stomping to the cadence of the shouts: Boom-Boom-BOOM! Boom-Boom-BOOM! Boom-Boom-BOOM!

The noise was so loud that the teacher across the hall called to the principal's office to get some support in their hallway before a riot broke out.

The assistant principal, Greg Upton, entered the classroom and shouted, "Hey! Hey! You little turds sit down and shut up! You're about to lose any privileges you have left. No school party! No school carnival. You won't even get to go to the library. Stop acting like the hoodlums you are, and start behaving like normal kids." He continued his rant for another several minutes and then grabbed Maxwell by the shirt collar.

"And you come with me," said Greg Upton. "You're suspended for three days." He dragged Maxwell out the door.

The students sat down in stunned silence.

Even Mrs. Owns had nothing to say. She turned her back to the class and slowly wrote on the board, "Please read pages 282 to 291 silently."

Mrs. Bradford, the principal, however, had plenty to say the next day.

She saw the entire incident unfold when she watched the video Carlos had taken with his mobile phone. No student was supposed to have a phone at the school during instructional time, but not only did Carlos manage to sneak his phone into the classroom, but he also captured the entire incident on video, from Maxwell's first statement about the "dead white guys" to Mr. Upton manhandling Maxwell and dragging him out of the classroom.

Normally, Mrs. Bradford wouldn't even have seen the video, but one of the third-grade teachers messaged her with a heads-up to take a look at the video. It was a good thing she had viewed it because, for the rest of the evening, her phone rang incessantly. Teachers and even friends were calling, and their conversations began with "Hey did you see . . . ?"

Mrs. Bradford had seen plenty. She already had had several discussions with Mr. Upton about automatically suspending students of color—without due process of any kind. When Mrs. Bradford looked over Mr. Upton's discipline data, she saw a definitive pattern. More black students than any other race had been suspended, and these students were predominantly male.

"Well, if the shoe fits . . . ," he had said in his defense.

"That's not how we show fairness and treat our students equally in this school, Mr. Upton," Mrs. Bradford had said. That had been six weeks before.

When Mrs. Bradford arrived at the school, she immediately went to Mr. Upton's office. His door was closed. She knocked, but there was no answer, so she wrote a note asking him to stop by her office when he arrived.

A half hour later, Mr. Upton knocked on the principal's door. He was carrying two cups of coffee, one of which was for Mrs. Bradford.

"I hope you don't mind that I'm a little late; I wanted to get some special coffee because today is going to be a great day. Maxwell has been suspended, and yes, you're welcome," said Mr. Upton.

"Mr. Upton, that is precisely what I want to talk to you about," said the principal. "I've seen the video, and so have most other people associated with our school."

"Video?" asked Mr. Upton.

3. Issue

Behavior management took a turn for the worse in a fifth-grade classroom. The students protested the lack of racially diverse authors in their reading textbooks, and in doing so, they nearly incited a riot.

One student took a video of the incident, even though students are not permitted to have mobile phones during instructional time at the campus.

The video showed that the assistant principal called students derogatory names and that he physically dragged one of the troublemakers out of the classroom and suspended him without due process.

4. Dilemma

Mrs. Bradford must decide how to handle several parts of this incident, including the assistant principal's actions, the students who misbehaved in class, the teacher who needed better classroom management skills, and the student who filmed (and posted) the video.

5. Questions

1. What should Mrs. Bradford do about Mr. Upton? What issues need to be addressed?
2. How should Mrs. Bradford handle Maxwell Black? Should she overturn the child's suspension? How can she involve the parents?
3. What punishment, if any, should Carlos receive for bringing his mobile phone to school? What about for uploading it to social media?
4. What should Mrs. Bradford do about Mrs. Owens and her discipline-management skill set?
5. How should the social media aspect of this case be handled?
6. Do you recommend that Mrs. Bradford drink the coffee?

―――❧❧❧――

1. They Read Just Fine

Grade Level: Urban Elementary School, Grades PK–5
Standards: 10c, e, School Improvement

2. Background

Principal Mark Roberts was excited that this would be the year he was adding a new teacher role to the faculty.

For several years now, the data he and his teachers collected showed two prominent trends at River Rock Elementary. The first was that reading scores were beginning to lag behind some of the other scores around the district. The scores hadn't actually plummeted—yet—but they were dropping several points each year.

There was reason for concern because his teachers were working harder than ever. He was in the classroom and saw their teaching. He helped his teachers with lesson plans when possible and even reviewed their assessments.

From what Mr. Roberts and the teachers could determine, the student population at River Rock Elementary was changing. Their percentage of English language learners (ELL) was up by 11 percent in the last year alone. The ELL students came from Mexico and several Muslim countries. Their first language was not English, and reading in any language had not been a priority. Getting to safety was far more important than learning.

Now in an American school for the first time, the foreign students were significantly underprepared for their studies.

Like his teachers, Principal Roberts knew that reading would be the key that unlocked these children's future. By learning how to read, especially in English, the students could learn a variety of other subjects, not just in elementary school, but also in middle school, high school, and beyond. Furthermore, many of the immigrant students would serve as translators for their parents, helping them acclimate to a new country even more quickly.

These teachers could not close the gaps by themselves, and this is where the reading specialist came in. She would work at catching the kids up so they wouldn't be behind.

At the school's PTA meeting in the cafeteria, Mr. Roberts introduced the new reading specialist, Mrs. Lindsey. He explained to the parents what her role at the campus would be. Primarily she would pull out those students needing the most reading intervention and help, work with them individually or in small groups, and send them back into their classrooms for the rest of their instruction.

"She'll begin by working with many of the immigrant students," said the principal. "English is a second or third language for them, and some of the students simply don't have the reading skills they need. We are going to help them catch up."

A murmur broke out across the audience. Several parents seemed to disagree with the arrangement Mr. Roberts had suggested.

Mr. Meyers stood up and yelled, "That ain't fair!"

Several of the parents turned around to look at him.

"You go and spend my tax dollars on something *my* kids don't get? What kind of system is that? Messed up, that's what that is," Mr. Meyers continued.

"Now please, Mr. Meyers," said Mr. Roberts. "Let's not assume anything. Of course any child who needs to see the reading specialist can see the reading specialist. Mrs. Lindsey will be helping students with their reading skills based on priority."

Several of the parents began filming the incident with their phones.

"You mean my kids come last?" asked Mr. Meyers. "Those other kids read just fine. They're lazy."

"No, not last. We are going to see to it that students with the greatest deficits are brought up to speed first. Mrs. Lindsey will see a variety of students throughout the year. Not just recent immigrants," said Mr. Roberts.

"Some immigrant comes before my kid? Or his kid? Or her kid?" Mr. Meyers jabbed his finger around the room. "No way!"

Mr. Davidson, another parent, stood up and cleared his throat. "You know, Mr. Meyers, we were, I believe, all immigrants in this country at one time. I myself am a third-generation immigrant, and someone made sure my family had what they needed to learn and grow and succeed in life. That is America."

"That is a load of garbage, Davidson. You make your own way, or you get out of the way. I don't want my money going to a bunch of immigrants. I'll bet most of them are here illegally. They shouldn't get a reading specialist. They oughtta be in special ed," said Mr. Meyers.

Mr. Roberts moved closer to the parent to calm him down. "Now, now, Mr. Meyers. Let's be rational here because . . ."

"*You* oughtta be in special ed!" yelled Mr. Davidson.

"Takes one to know one!" shouted Mr. Meyers.

"You wouldn't know compassion, decency, or even intelligence if you tripped over them," said Mr. Davidson.

He no sooner said the words when Mr. Meyers pulled back his right arm and let fly a punch.

Everyone could hear the sound of bone crunching, and they winced collectively. Mr. Davidson was still standing, and he seemed fine.

Then they noticed who was missing. Mr. Roberts had fallen to the ground, and he held his hands over his nose.

Mr. Meyers had hit the principal squarely in the face, and parents were uploading their videos of the whole thing on social media sites.

3. Issue

River Rock Elementary has acquired a reading specialist to work with a changing population.

When the teacher was introduced at a PTA meeting, one parent became argumentative and publicly put down immigrants. When another parent tried to calm him down, the first parent pulled a punch and assaulted the school principal.

Other parents filmed the incident and posted it on social media.

4. Dilemma

Mr. Roberts, the school principal at River Rock Elementary, has a volatile situation on his hands. Several of the parents are upset about the hiring of a reading specialist to help immigrant students close their gaps in reading.

One of the parents has hit the principal, knocking him down and likely breaking his nose. Video of the incident has been uploaded onto social media platforms.

5. Questions

1. Should Mr. Roberts have introduced the role of the reading specialist at this meeting?

2. Should he have mentioned which students would be identified first for reading intervention?

3. When should Mr. Roberts have stopped Mr. Meyers from speaking? What should he have said?

4. What are Mr. Roberts's next steps? Can he have Mr. Meyers removed from the campus?

5. How should the uploads to social media be handled? How should Mr. Meyers be handled?

1. Change Begins Now

Grade Level: Suburban Elementary School, Grades PK–5
Standards: 10i, j, School Improvement

2. Background

Clark King brought his first box of personal items to his new office. He had just been appointed the new principal at Sweetwater Elementary.

The assignment was a dream come true for Mr. King. He had been the first to go to college in his family, and he became a science teacher. He was pretty good at it, too, because, within several years of teaching, he was recognized as the teacher of the year at his campus and then district-wide.

His administrators had seen another talent in Mr. King, and they encouraged him to go back to school to get a degree in educational administration. Mr. King worked hard and became an assistant principal. He wasn't fond of supervising "books, butts, and buses," but he was good at it.

He developed a textbook inventory system for his campus that was adopted district-wide. He went to the halls to handle discipline rather than have students lined up outside his office, and there were no safety incidents to report regarding transportation. He could have had a good career as an assistant principal, but he knew he had more to offer.

When the position at Sweetwater opened up, Mr. King applied for it immediately. He wanted this campus—it had a good faculty, and the parents were involved in their children's education. He had an interview, crossed his fingers, and waited.

Now he would be the principal at Sweetwater Elementary, and he was tremendously excited about getting to lead his own campus.

The outgoing principal, Emma Gonzalez, had been at Sweetwater Elementary for more than a decade. She greeted Mr. King aloofly and pointed to an office where he could set up.

"That's the assistant principal's office," said Mr. King.

"Yes, it is," said Mrs. Gonzalez. "It's the only empty one available right now, so it will have to do."

"But I'm not an AP—I'm coming in as the new principal," said Mr. King.

"And I haven't left the building yet. My last day isn't for another three weeks."

Mr. King took his box into the vacant office. There really was no reason to unpack it if he would have to move everything again in three weeks. He could use the time now to become familiar with other things at the campus.

A few days later, Mrs. Gonzalez came to him and said, "Hey, want a free lunch this Friday?"

"Um, okay," Mr. King replied.

"One of the textbook companies is offering a free lunch. All you have to do is listen to a short presentation. They usually have some great door prizes, too. I go all the time. Usually several times a month," said Mrs. Gonzalez.

Mr. King felt slightly uncomfortable, but he agreed to go. Just this once, he told himself.

On Friday, Mrs. Gonzalez stood in the doorway of Mr. King's temporary office.

"C'mon, you can follow me," she said. "I'm going home afterward, but you probably ought to come back to work."

Neither principal won a door prize, but Mrs. Gonzalez had several glasses of wine at the luncheon.

"What are they going to do, fire me?" she asked no one in particular. Then she laughed too loudly.

The next week at the campus, Mrs. Gonzalez began packing her things in boxes. She was in no hurry, however, so Mr. King occupied himself with other things.

As the teachers came into the building to prepare their classrooms, he meet with each one, asking what should stay the same and what one thing should change. The teachers said that one thing was being changed by getting a new principal.

A week before the teachers were to return, they invited Mr. King and Mrs. Gonzalez to a Saturday cookout in one of the nearby parks. Mrs. Gonzalez declined, but Mr. King went. He played tag football, ate hamburgers, drank at least a gallon (it seemed) of iced tea, and threw a Frisbee with several of the teachers' kids.

The teachers had plenty of questions for Mr. King. What changes did he want to see at the school? *See that teachers have the supplies and support they need to do their jobs.* What did he think of the new reading program the district adopted? *Early to tell, but it seemed like it could be a good fit for their students.* How did he feel about sending kids to the office for discipline? *Better to be visible so huge discipline problems don't develop.*

Then the conversation turned more personal. Was he married? *Not yet.* Did he one day want to be a superintendent? *That's too far in the future to decide. For now, the goal is to be a great principal.* What did he do for fun? *Read, take his dogs for walks, go to work.*

The teachers loved what they saw in their new principal, and they wasted no time in telling the other teachers that Mr. King was like a breath of fresh air. They lit up social media with their perception of their new boss.

The teachers couldn't wait to start the year.

Neither could Mr. King, now that he was in the principal's office. Mrs. Gonzalez had just left the day before, so Mr. King finally could hang his framed degrees on the wall and set a few items on his desk.

Several of the third-grade teachers stopped by the office.

"It looks good in here," they observed. "Do you have some time to listen to some ideas?"

"Thanks. And of course. Let me just finish this," said Mr. King as he placed a framed picture next to the books on the shelf behind his desk.

He turned around to see the expression on the teachers' faces. They kept looking at the picture of Mr. King and what was obviously his boyfriend.

"You're . . . *gay?*" they asked.

3. Issue

Mr. King is the new principal at Sweetwater Elementary, but the leaving principal, Mrs. Gonzalez, has not left the principal's office yet. She makes him take an assistant's office instead of yielding her space to him.

Mrs. Gonzalez invites Mr. King to go to a luncheon put on by a textbook company. She drinks several glasses of wine and goes home for the day, but he doesn't say anything.

When the teachers invite the two principals for a Saturday outing, Mr. King attends, but Mrs. Gonzalez does not. The teachers have plenty of questions for Mr. King, which he answers.

4. Dilemma

Mr. King did not tell the district about Mrs. Gonzalez's lunches. Instead he focused on building positive relationships with his faculty. When he was finally able to move into the principal's office, he displayed personal items, including a picture of himself and his boyfriend.

The third-grade teachers are the first to discover that Mr. King has a boyfriend when he displays a picture of the two of them on the bookshelf in his office.

5. Questions

1. Should Mr. King have demanded that he be allowed to take the principal's office immediately? Why or why not?
2. What should Mr. King begin familiarizing himself with while Mrs. Gonzalez is still in the principal's office?
3. Should Mr. King say anything about the wine Mrs. Gonzalez had at lunch—or who paid for the lunch?
4. What should Mr. King tell the third-grade teachers about his private life?
5. Do you recommend that Mr. King display the photograph? Why or why not?

Chapter Three

Multicultural Issues and Cultural Competence

—◦◦◦—

1. Ticket to Fun

Grade Level: Urban Elementary School, Grades PK–5
Standards: 3a, d, e, Equity and Cultural Responsiveness

2. Background

Polk Elementary was in the process of transitioning their behavior management approach from a punitive to a positive system.

The previous principal, Rex Rogers, believed in identifying bad behavior early and doling out heavy consequences for it. He didn't believe in timeouts, preferred out-of-school suspensions, and had no tolerance for students who repeatedly broke the school rules.

It seemed as though the students who were always in trouble came from one particular neighborhood—Pinnacle Point. Ironically, this neighborhood had been developed in the lowest area of the city. It seemed as though every road to Pinnacle went downhill. Pinnacle Point was at the outer edge of the school attendance zone; it was a collection of multifamily structures and was known for cheap rent, transient families, and high crime.

The students were also predominantly of minority ethnicities.

"No wonder these snots are always in trouble," said Mr. Rogers. "They can't help themselves. It's all they know how to do, so we are going to punish them for their behavior. They are going to learn wrong from right, at least while they are with us."

Mr. Rogers hired many teachers during his tenure at Polk Elementary who felt similarly about handling bad behavior with punitive consequences. Many felt that corporal punishment was the best solution to their problems.

Mr. Rogers agreed, but he pointed out that that consequence had been stripped from them.

"That isn't going to stop us from stopping those kids, especially the ones from Pinnacle Point."

The teachers used a three-strike approach. At the first infraction, the student's name went on the board, with a checkmark next to the student's name for each following infraction. Some teacher were so frustrated with the student behaviors that they placed checkmark after checkmark by the students' names. Soon it became a game to see how quickly the students could make their teachers angry.

Mrs. Bidwell was perhaps the angriest teacher of all. When Jackson Brown refused to stop standing on his desk during class, his teacher placed big Xs next to Jackson's name on the board. Then she drew small skulls above the marks.

"That's a good one," laughed Principal Rogers when he walked into the room and saw what the teacher had done. "All right, Jackson, you're outta here. Don't make me call security." Then the principal called Jackson profane names based on the child's race.

Jackson wasn't the only one who was "outta there." LaWonda Jones filmed the incident on her mobile phone and posted the video on a social media site.

When the superintendent found out, he placed Mr. Rogers on administrative leave and placed an interim principal, Sherry Luhan, at Polk Elementary.

Principal Luhan's first order of business was to change the Polk discipline program, but she'd also have to change the attitudes of many the teachers who worked there. At her first faculty meeting with the teachers, she presented them with data from various discipline programs. She showed the effectiveness of each one with student populations similar to the one they taught at Polk.

Next, Luhan asked the teachers which program they would like to implement.

"The one we have," said Mrs. Bidwell under her breath.

"It's important that the approach we select aligns with what we know about child development.," said Mrs. Luhan. After further discussion, the staff reluctantly agreed to try positive behavior supports. Rather than penalize students for their behavior, they would try to find the good in every student and celebrate it.

They met several more times to determine which behaviors they wanted to see in their students and how the students would be rewarded.

"How about they get to stay in school," said Mrs. Bidwell. "Why do we have to reward them for doing something they are supposed to do anyway?"

"For the same reason you like getting treats and even bonuses," said Mrs. Luhan.

Again the teachers worked on levels of incentives. They created behavior tickets that students could use to purchase treats on special days or special events like the school carnival.

The students responded well to the ticket system, and they liked getting to purchase items with their earned tickets. These items consisted of useful items like special school supplies and even treats, like chocolate.

A journal or a glitter pen cost one ticket. Novelty pencils, sharpeners, and crayons cost two tickets. A small piece of chocolate cost three tickets.

The ticket system generated new excitement among the students about the upcoming carnival. Playing each game at the school carnival would cost a predetermined number of tickets, and students could buy refreshments for themselves and their families with their tickets.

"You're not letting the kids from Pinnacle Point come, are you?" asked Mrs. Bidwell. Every time they show up, there's trouble."

"All students who have earned tickets for their good behavior are welcome at the school carnival," said Mrs. Luhan.

"Oh, I can fix that," said Mrs. Bidwell.

3. Issue

The former principal, Rex Rogers, perpetuated an outdated behavior-management system based on punitive measures, many of which targeted students of color from a particular neighborhood. When he was placed on leave because of inappropriate comments, Mrs. Bidwell vowed to maintain the status quo and keep Mr. Rogers's vision alive.

When the interim principal brought in a new system, Mrs. Bidwell refused to implement it.

All of the other teachers in Mrs. Bidwell's grade rewarded students with tickets for their good behavior. The students began to understand which behaviors the teachers wanted to see more of, and they chose the behaviors that would earn them more coveted tickets.

Mrs. Bidwell, however, refused to reward her students with tickets.

"Hey, that's not fair," said Jackson.

"I'm not here to be fair," said Mrs. Bidwell. No students in her room earned tickets. She refused to give them out.

4. Dilemma

With the school carnival just around the corner, students were eagerly trying to earn as many tickets as they could. They wanted to come to the event, play games, and enjoy some of the treats.

One week before the school carnival, several parents wanted to meet with interim principal Sherry Luhan. They were from Pinnacle Point, and they wanted to know why their children had not earned any tickets for their behavior. LaWonda and Jackson were with them.

"Yeah," they said. "Mrs. Bidwell won't give any of us tickets. Not even when I don't stand on my desk. She says we're not good enough to get them."

The parents wanted to know how Mrs. Luhan planned to resolve this dilemma.

5. Questions

1. Should Mr. Rogers have been placed on administrative leave for his comments? What consequences, if any, should Mrs. Bidwell face for drawing skulls next to a student's name?
2. What did the interim principal do correctly in adopting a new behavior system? What areas could she have worked harder at?
3. What sort of follow-up was needed regarding the new ticket system?
4. What should Mrs. Luhan do about Mrs. Bidwell's comments? What about her refusal to distribute tickets to students for good behavior or her targeting students from a particular neighborhood?
5. How should Mrs. Luhan handle the situation with the angry parents?

1. Rainy Day Recess

Grade Level: Rural Elementary School, Grades PK–5
Standards: 3b, Equity and Cultural Responsiveness; 8b, Meaningful Engagement of Families and Community

2. Background

Cook Elementary was a small school in a rural area. Because the district didn't have a lot of resources, the campuses did the best they could with limited supplies and materials. The teachers didn't always have everything they wanted, but they felt they had everything they needed.

The parents and the community helped out where they could. The local grocery partnered with the school, providing snacks for big school parties, and the only fast food restaurant in the area offered junior kids' meals as an incentive for students who had perfect attendance at the end of the year.

The building itself was the biggest challenge at Cook Elementary. The school had a small cafeteria and a sufficient library, and every classroom was in use. The only thing that Cook Elementary didn't have was a gym.

On most days, the lack of a gymnasium was not a problem. The children had PE outside. When it was hot, the PE teacher made use of the covered pavilion, which was a flat metal roof suspended over a large concrete slab. The pavilion was large enough to house a basketball hoop at either end.

During free time on Fridays, the kids shot hoops, played tag and hopscotch, and drew in colored chalk on the concrete. The school encouraged the children to express themselves in their play.

It was a problem when it rained.

The children couldn't play in the pavilion when it rained because the concrete got wet from blowing rain, so they had to have PE indoors. Sometimes it was possible to use the cafeteria for PE—if there wasn't something else planned in that space or if it wasn't lunchtime. Lunch trumped everything.

Principal Wallace's solution was simple.

On those days that the rain kept students indoors, the teachers would have to supervise their play in the classroom. The PE teacher visited the classrooms to help with supervision and give the teachers a short break to take care of personal needs.

Students couldn't engage in physical exercise in the classrooms. With the desks and chairs, there wasn't much room to move around. Instead, every teacher had alternative activities planned. Creative Days, as they were called, were designed by the teachers.

In some of the classes, teachers permitted the children to draw or color, and in others, they worked on reading and math skills on one of the two computers in each classroom. Many of the teachers set up centers, turned on a timer, and let the students rotate through each station.

Miss Woodward was a new teacher at Cook Elementary, and she proved herself to be exceptionally creative and daring in her activities.

Miss Woodward's students worked in centers that were quite diverse. At one center was a container of Legos. Painting and dancing took up space at other centers. Miss Woodward also had a big trunk filled with all kinds of clothing.

During her years in college, Miss Woodward had been in theater, and as a result, she discovered that she loved costuming. Whenever she found an interesting piece at a thrift store or that was being thrown out, she added it to her collection.

The trunk contained a variety of hats, several shirts and jackets, trousers, and even a couple of organza skirts in bright colors. There was a yellow tutu, a red feather boa, and even a plastic sword that the children loved playing with.

Principal Wallace felt that Miss Woodward's classroom was remarkably encouraging. It was a place where children could explore and have fun. They really seemed to look forward to Creative Days.

Jason Dodd, a student in Miss Woodward's class, especially seemed to enjoy Creative Days. He liked to begin at the costume center, and whatever he picked out to wear that day, he wanted to wear to all the other centers. Miss Woodward had no problem with that. In her mind, it was completely natural to see a sword-wielding pirate pretending to work on a rocket engine.

The pirate outfit, however, was not Jason's favorite costume. His favorite outfit was the yellow tutu, the red feather boa, and a cowboy hat. He especially liked to twirl and twirl and twirl around in the tutu, his arms over his head like a ballerina.

It was in the middle of one of these twirls that Jason's father walked into Miss Woodward's classroom. He had stopped by to drop off his son's scouting materials for the meeting after school that day. Principal Wallace had told Mr. Dodd that the children were in the classroom for Creative Day because of the rain; Mr. Dodd was welcome to just drop in.

At first, Mr. Dodd couldn't believe his eyes. His voice boomed across the room. "What in the world, Sam?"

"Dad!" said Jason, freezing in place. "What are you doing here?"

"The question is what are *you* doing?" Then Mr. Dodd turned to Miss Woodward. "Can you please tell me why it's okay for my son to dress like a girl and act like some kind of sissy-boy?"

Miss Woodward stood up. "Mr. Dodd, I didn't think—"

"No, you sure didn't. What kind of fruit loop teacher are you, anyway?" asked Mr. Dodd. "I'll tell you what kind. The fired kind because I'm going to have your job."

Miss Woodward ran from the classroom in tears.

3. Issue

The physical limitations of the school building have forced Principal Wallace and his teachers to turn to creative solutions during PE when the weather is inclement. Each teacher has been allowed to design his or her Creative Days activities in the classroom.

One teacher in particular encourages creative play that is non–gender specific. One of the boys likes to dress in girl's clothing, and his father catches him in the act when he walks into the classroom to drop off materials for a later meeting.

4. Dilemma

The parent, Mr. Dodd, threatens to get the teacher fired because she has allowed his son to wear feminine clothing and dance like a ballerina. The teacher leaves the classroom in tears, with only the parent, who dropped by unannounced, to supervise.

The principal, Mr. Wallace, had always been hugely supportive of Miss Woodward's teaching practices, but the parent's attitude may make him change his mind.

5. Questions

1. What might have been a better way to spend Creative Days to meet the requirements of PE?
2. Should Mr. Wallace permit Miss Woodward to continue her activities for Creative Days?
3. What should Miss Woodward have done instead of running from the classroom?
4. How can Mr. Wallace handle Mr. Dodd's threat to the teacher?
5. What suggestions might Mr. Wallace make to the district about the pavilion?

1. Bullying on the Bus

Grade Level: Urban Elementary School, Grades 1–5
Standards: 3a, d, g, Equity and Cultural Responsiveness; 5e, Community of Care and Support for Students

2. Background

Booker T. Washington Elementary is an urban campus for public school students in grades 1 to 5. The school has long been a part of the bustling city community, and alums of this prestigious campus include the mayor and several prominent businessmen and businesswomen. These community leaders came from humble backgrounds and credit Booker T. Washington Elementary for laying a strong foundation educationally and emotionally for their future success.

Known and respected for its ability to demonstrate equity and cultural responsiveness, Booker T. Washington Elementary has several high-profile students of various ethnic backgrounds attending this year. Several of the school district's principals have placed their children at the campus, and so has the superintendent of schools. In addition, the news anchor's daughter attends this school.

Students who are not as high profile as those mentioned are treated with the same respect as everyone else. That's also true for ethnicity. African Americans, Hispanics, and whites, who make up 95 percent of the student population, get along with each other for the most part.

Occasional feuds arise when tempers flare, but common sense often prevails. Most students settle back into their routines, although there has been an uptick in name-calling and posturing in the hallways.

Most of the faculty thought these behaviors were due to the nearness of the holidays. Everyone was ready for a break.

Naturally, it came as a surprise when Keylie Pirani's parent came to the school for a meeting with the administration. The serious look on the faces of the parents told Ms. Shalindra Jackson, the principal, that something very wrong had happened.

Ms. Jackson had no idea how right she was.

Although Booker T. Washington Elementary was ethnically diverse, Keylie was the first Muslim student to attend this school. She was an English language learner in the fifth grade. English was Keylie's third language; she also spoke Arabic and French. Keylie's English was weak, however, and she was also a poor reader who struggled to keep up in class. She had decided on her own that she wanted to wear her traditional scarf, the hijab, to school.

Keylie's teacher had recommended her for the after-school tutoring program, but Keylie never stayed. Instead, she rode the bus home.

As days turned into weeks, the unusually quiet and soft-spoken Keylie became even more introverted. She ran directly to her bedroom when she arrived home at the end of a school day and muttered something about having a ton of homework to do. She would lie on her bed and sob until dinner was ready.

At first, her parents thought her crying was because of the amount of homework and the possibility that she was not able to keep up in English with her peers. When they were finally able to get the truth, they learned that Keylie was being bullied at school and especially on the bus.

The insults included taunts like "piranha-face," camel-spit," and "sand-sucker." Keylie was careful to pronounce the words correctly so her parents would understand them.

She told how two boys on the bus taunted her the most. They took pictures of her without her permission, and they posted them on Internet sites such as Snapchat, where pictures and texts are not saved automatically. Snaps completely disappear, even from the servers, after twenty-four hours.

When asked how she knew this about the pictures in Snapchat, Keylie said, "Easy. Michelle told me. She even showed me one or two on her phone before they disappeared." Michelle was one of Keylie's only two friends at school. She was also the daughter of the PTA president. The other friend was Olivia, the daughter of the local news anchor.

Mr. Pirani's anger grew until clenching and unclenching his fists would not release the tension that was building up.

He turned away from Keylie and punched a hole in the wall.

"No, Daddy, no!" Keylie cried. Then she cowered.

Mr. Pirani turned back to his daughter. "I am not mad at you, my dear. I am angry at whoever could do this to you. We will not let it continue."

Mr. Pirani thought for a moment. "Don't you have a friend whose mother is the news anchor? Perhaps she would like to report on an interesting story."

Tears began to fall from Keylie's eyes again. She had left out the part where she spat on the boys when they bullied her. She didn't know whether to tell her dad.

The next day, the Piranis went to Booker T. Washington Elementary to meet with Principal Jackson.

3. Issue

The Piranis were the first to alert Ms. Jackson of the incidents that had taken place.

After listening to their detailed account of what had been happening on the bus—and possibly even in the school—Ms. Jackson felt that Keylie was the victim of bullying. Not only had she been called horrible names and slurs, but other students regularly grabbed Keylie's hijab, threw it on the bus floor, and trampled it before throwing it back at her. They took pictures of Keylie and posted them on Snapchat.

The bus driver never reported any of these incidents, and neither did the other students.

4. Dilemma

After conducting a thorough investigation into the matter, Ms. Jackson has discovered that one of the students who bullied Keylie is the son of the PTA president at the school. The other bully is the superintendent's son. Although several other students also participated in the bullying, the first two mentioned were the instigators.

She learned that Keylie spat on the boys *before* they insulted her.

Both Michelle and Olivia knew about the pictures and messages that appeared on Snapchat but said nothing about them because the photos were always gone by the time they got the courage to speak up. They did not know that Keylie spat on the boys first.

The Piranis are now in Ms. Jackson's office again, and this time they are demanding Ms. Jackson take immediate action. They want to know what the principal plans to do about the bullying. How will she make it stop? They also want to know exactly what the consequences are for each of the bullies. They want this information in a letter signed by the principal and the superintendent.

"If I do not have this letter in three days," warned Mr. Pirani, "an attorney from CAIR [Council on American Islamic Relations] will contact you."

5. Questions

1. What, if any, consequences should Keylie face for spitting on the boys?
2. What documents or other proof can Ms. Jackson gather to prove what has happened?
3. What actions, if any, should she take against the sons of the PTA president and the superintendent?
4. Should Ms. Jackson detail the consequences the boys are facing and give the letter to Mr. Pirani? Why or why not?
5. What follow-up do you recommend Ms. Jackson provide for the student population and faculty?

1. Sanctuary School

Grade Level: Urban Elementary School, Grades PK–5
Standards: 3a, c, g, Equity and Cultural Responsiveness

2. Background

Mr. Cruz made it clear to his faculty at their afternoon faculty meeting that Cesar Chavez Elementary would follow their superintendent's directions regarding ICE (Immigration and Customs Enforcement) and the possible roundup of immigrants.

The whole immigration issue had been on every news station, and it was also a hot topic on social media.

Superintendent Alba Lozano announced earlier that day in a meeting with the principals that the La Primavera Public School District would be following in the footsteps of the Chicago Public Schools (CPS). The CPS superintendent directed the principals in Chicago to forbid ICE or other law enforcement officials from entering the schools within their system without a warrant. They would not suffer any child (or adult) to be arrested if they were within the confines of the building.

If law enforcement showed up on the campus, then the police would have to wait outside while the school principal contacted the school district's attorney for legal counsel. In short, every school, its faculty, and its staff was to act as a sanctuary for immigrants of any kind.

The school district took this stance because of the newly elected president's remarks about illegal immigration. President Donald J. Trump said he wanted to build a wall between Mexico and the United States and that he also wanted to deport illegal immigrants with criminal records.

Principal Cruz handed out a letter to his faculty and staff.

"You may have already read this letter, but I wanted you to have a copy for yourselves," he said. "This is the letter we sent home today to the parents of all students in the school. You'll see that it is in English on one side and Spanish on the other side."

The letter read:

Dear Parents and Families,

By now you may have heard that U.S. Immigration and Customs Enforcement (ICE) have been authorized to detain and even arrest persons who may have had a questionable background regarding immigration to our country.

We understand the fear and anxiety that their presence may cause you, particularly because there are rumors of students being detained while at school. Some of the stories going around have included tales that entire families are being split apart because of one family member being arrested and deported.

The La Primavera Public School District wants you to know that you and your children will be safe while you are on any of our campuses or within any of our schools. We do not expect that ICE agents will come to arrest and deport anyone, but if they do, be assured that we have a safety plan in place for you and especially for your children.

We will provide awareness sessions on this matter, but for now, please refer to this handy card that tells you what to do in the event that ICE stops you when you are not in a location designated as a sanctuary. In the meantime, be assured that your confidential information, such as your physical address, will remain confidential, and we will be on our guard to protect your children.

Viva la Raza!
Best regards,
Alba Lozano, Superintendent of Schools

The accompanying card explained what an immigrant should do if accosted by law enforcement. Suggestions included obeying laws to avoid being noticed, denying ICE entrance without a warrant, and creating a safety plan in the event of arrest. La Primavera Public School District modeled their flyer after the Chicago Public Schools' palm card.

"Any questions?" asked the principal.

"Yeah, I'm not sure if it's a question as much as a statement," said Mrs. Barbara Jackson.

"Go ahead," said Mr. Cruz.

"Just why in the world am I supposed to harbor criminals in my classroom or in my school?" the teacher asked. "I am sick and tired of all of our resources going to people who aren't even citizens. Don't we have enough need in our own community without getting freeloaders from other countries? Plus, these immigrants are here illegally. Many of them have committed crimes, and some of them have been dreadful. They need to go back to wherever they came from."

The assistant principal tried to hush Mrs. Jackson, but Mr. Cruz waved him away.

"Let her speak her mind," he said.

When Mrs. Jackson finished several minutes later, she took a deep breath and sat down. Some of the teachers gave her thumbs up, and some of them tried to inch their chairs a little further away from where Mrs. Jackson was sitting.

Clearly, the faculty was ready to take sides on this issue. You could feel iciness from the teachers on both sides of the issue.

"All right, it's my turn," said Mr. Cruz.

The principal turned to address the faculty regarding the issue.

3. Issue

The La Primavera Public School District has decided to pattern its stance in the immigration issue on that of the Chicago Public Schools, which determined that every school within its district would be a sanctuary campus that would keep children safe from arrest and deportation.

The La Primavera Public School District superintendent asked that every campus send a explanatory letter home to parents and that the principals review the letter's contents with their faculties.

Not every faculty member agrees with the school system's decision, and the faculty has quickly taken sides.

4. Dilemma

One teacher has spoken up regarding her position on immigration and having sanctuary schools that protect illegal immigrants. Her rant has divided the faculty into opposing factions. Principal Cruz has received a directive from the superintendent of schools; he must follow it. He must also try to unite the faculty on this issue, or no children will feel safe in the school.

5. Questions

1. What should Principal Cruz tell his faculty after Mrs. Jackson spoke? What would you say if you were in his shoes?
2. What in the superintendent's letter was well said? What should have been written differently?
3. Can a school be a sanctuary for immigrants?
4. If you were the principal at Cesar Chavez Elementary and immigrant parents decided to remain in the school's parent center, what would you do?
5. How would you handle a phone call from ICE? What if it was from the media?

1. Not in My Classroom

Grade Level: Rural Elementary School, Grades PK–5
Standards: 3f, g, Equity and Cultural Responsiveness

2. Background

Mrs. Letty Longmire has been teaching second grade for several years. She had tried fifth grade once and found that she couldn't handle the students, and students in kindergarten and first grade were too "needy," as she put it.

It turned out that second grade was a good fit—she could handle student behavior without a problem, and she was excellent in instructional delivery. Her lessons came alive through thematic inclusion, where she could combine teaching several subjects.

Mrs. Longmire's classroom was a safe place for students, and they liked being there. Part of the charm of being in class with Mrs. Longmire was that she was deeply compassionate, a characteristic she attributes to her faith. She is a practicing and devout Christian.

On several occasions, the principal, Mrs. Mary Judson, has had to ask Mrs. Longmire to remove certain posters form her classroom. These posters had overtly religious themes and references to Christianity, including some with Bible verses on them.

When Mrs. Judson asked that the posters be removed, Mrs. Longmire complied. After a few weeks, another one would go up in its place. Mrs. Longmire also had several affirmations of faith on her desk, including a family photo in which several members are holding their Bibles. In addition, Mrs. Longmire has a small calendar near her desk; this calendar shows a different Bible verse for each day of the week.

As soon as she saw these affirmations, Mrs. Judson asked Mrs. Longmire to remove them.

The principal also met with the teacher afterward in the office.

"I, too, am a Christian," said Mrs. Judson, "but Bible verses and other outright signs of Christianity do not belong in the classroom. We have to remain neutral in our religious beliefs while at school because of the separation of church and state."

"It's not right," said Mrs. Longmire. "Most of the kids in class come from Christian families."

"This is true," said Mrs. Judson, "but not all of them do. There are families—the Feinbergs and the Gibrans, for example—who may find the verses offensive. You also have a student in your classroom whose parents are atheists."

"All the more reason to have scripture in the classroom," said Mrs. Longmire.

"Mrs. Longmire," said Principal Judson, "I think you are a very good teacher. You are loving and compassionate. And you can teach without these materials on the walls and desk in your classroom. My directive to you is to remove and stop putting them back up."

Mrs. Longmire indicated that she understood the directive, and she left the principal's office. She went to her room and removed everything related to religion.

When the next six-week instructional period began, all of the teachers in second grade prepared for a unit related to history and social studies. The unit centered on important religions of the world. Its objective was to show how world religions helped to form cultures.

They would teach about Buddhism, Christianity, Hinduism, Islam, and Judaism—in alphabetical order so as not to show preference for one religion over another. All of the teachers were excited about the lessons and activities. All of them, that is, except Mrs. Longmire. She had been unusually quiet.

When the new six weeks began, the teachers introduced the religion, showed its geographic birthplace, and talked about important leaders of the religion. They also showed students what the followers of each religion believed and how those beliefs affected the world around them. To connect with literature, the teachers had students read folktales and literature from each culture.

Principal Judson made regular observations in each of the second-grade teachers' classrooms, but she wasn't always present for social studies. In the first four of the six weeks, she had observed the social studies class only once. Mrs. Longmire hadn't seemed overly excited about the lesson she was teaching, but Mrs. Judson didn't think anything of it.

When Islam week came up, the teachers showed their students how to pray through preparation, kneeling, and reciting passages from the Quran. To help them with their learning, the teachers sent the prayers home with students. They could practice them for homework.

The next day, one of the teachers brought Mrs. Judson the homework from one of her students. Scrawled across the top in large red letters were the words "MY CHILD WILL NOT DO THIS ASSIGNMENT." Several of the other teachers had similar experiences, with parents refusing to practice the prayer verse from Islam. Some parents added a note requesting that their child be transferred to Mrs. Longmire's class.

Mrs. Judson called the parents to inform them that an assignment given by a teacher must be done for homework. The verse and the prayer were part of the curriculum developed by the district, which certainly knew what it was doing when showing how the five religions were similar and different. She saw nothing wrong with the assignment, and neither should the parents. No transfer requests would be honored.

Mrs. Judson went to observe the lessons being taught in each of the second-grade classrooms. She took the scope and sequence with her. Each teacher was teaching the unit on religion exactly as had been outlined in the district plan for instruction. The students in the classes were memorizing and practicing the Islamic prayer; it was even displayed on the wall.

The only teacher who was doing something different was Mrs. Longmire. There was no practicing, and there was no prayer posted on the wall for the students to see. The students were seated quietly at their desks, coloring a map of countries that practiced Islam.

"Why aren't your students practicing the prayer, Mrs. Longmire?" asked the principal.

"You have directed me that there is a separation of church and state, Mrs. Judson. If you are asking me to teach the children to pray, you may contact my attorney."

3. Issue

Several times Mrs. Judson has had to reprimand Mrs. Longmire for displaying Christian memorabilia and Bible verses in her classroom.

The second-grade curriculum developed by the district requires the teacher to introduce the five most practiced religions, showing how each religion affects cultures and civilizations around the world.

Only Mrs. Longmire does not teach the unit on Islam the way the district prescribed, which is to have the children recite an Islamic prayer on their knees. No other religion taught included instruction in prayer.

Several of the parents are furious about the assignment.

Mrs. Longmire has told the principal that she refuses to teach the prayer, having been directed to remove Bible quotes from the walls of her classroom.

4. Dilemma

Mrs. Judson has tried to create a separation of church and state in her school. When Mrs. Longmire displayed Christian symbols and items in her classroom, Mrs. Judson directed the second-grade teacher to remove them.

Furthermore, the principal denied parent requests to stop the Islamic prayer assignment or to transfer students to Mrs. Longmire's classroom, saying that the district knows what it's doing with the curriculum.

Mrs. Longmire has demonstrated insubordination by refusing to teach the curriculum the way it was intended and has threatened to involve an attorney in the matter.

5. Questions

1. What is the leader's responsibility for creating cohesiveness in this situation?
2. Was it appropriate to ask Mrs. Longmire to remove the Christian memorabilia and Bible verse posters from her classroom? Why or why not? *Is* there a time that the Bible can be used in instruction?
3. Was Mrs. Judson right in backing up the district regarding implementation of the social studies scope and sequence? Why or why not?
4. What would have been a better way to handle the irate parents?
5. What should Mrs. Judson do if the parents take to social media and begin posting their complaints?
6. How appropriate was the alternative activity given in Mrs. Longmire's class? Why?
7. Is Mrs. Longmire's final statement insubordination? Why or why not?

1. Left Behind

Grade Level: Rural Elementary School, Grades PK–5
Standards: 5a, b, c, Community of Care and Support for Students

2. Background

The bus routes for each of the campuses in Springfield Independent School District were some of the longest in the state due to the expansiveness of the district. At two hundred square miles, the district covered a huge part of the state. So did the bus routes.

Students rode for thirty to forty minutes on the bus, sometimes longer, whether going to or from school. The buses traveled across paved farm-to-market roads as well as dirt roads lined with little more than years of dust.

Sometimes the students read or completed their homework on the trip. They listened to music. They even slept, especially the younger students at the end of the school day.

When the drivers completed their routes, they headed back to the bus barn. One of their final duties was to walk the aisles of the buses to make sure nothing and no one was left behind.

The long bus routes were the toughest for the younger elementary students, who weren't used to a long day at school and another long ride home. Parents put a lot of trust in the school bus drivers to get their little ones home safely. The schools did its part in making sure students got on the right bus at the end of each day.

Vanessa Cantu, the principal at Grove Elementary, had heard stories from other principals about transportation routes gone wrong. Bus drivers got lost, and parents panicked; the first two weeks of school were always busy, as the office fielded phone calls from parents who were worried that the bus had forgotten to pick up or drop off their children.

Ms. Cantu decided that this year she and her teachers would help the new students get used to the bus routes. She requested that teams of teachers ride the bus routes home with the students for the first week of school. Doing so would serve several purposes. First, the bus drivers would have additional supervision while transporting the students. Second, the faculty and staff would ensure that the students got to the right house. And finally, the teachers would learn a lot about where their students lived and the kind of environments they lived in.

Ms. Cantu, her two assistant principals, the counselors, and the librarian would also ride a bus. The principal wanted to ride each of the buses so she would know where her children were from and she could meet the parents along each route.

After obtaining permission from the transportation department, Ms. Cantu explained her plan to the teachers. Not everyone shared her excitement about riding the buses. Some of the teachers could not devote the time it would take after school.

The first week of school arrived, and Ms. Cantu and the faculty ended each instructional day by boarding the buses and riding the route to the homes and back again to the campus. By the end of the week, the teachers and administrators were exhausted, but they agreed the experience had been great. The parents were happy to see such caring teachers, too, and they clearly appreciated the efforts the educators had taken. They made many great comments in social media about the gesture.

The next couple of weeks went well, until the Thursday that kindergartner Tyler Compton did not get off the bus at the end of the day.

Ms. Cantu happened to be working late that day. An hour after the school day ended, the parents called to report that Tyler had not returned home. Ms. Cantu called the bus barn and verified that the driver was still en route. She called the Comptons back to let them know their son would be home soon.

Another thirty minutes went by, and the Comptons called again to say that Tyler had not gotten home.

Ms. Cantu called the bus barn again. The driver had returned the bus and clocked out some time ago.

"There's no way," said Ms. Cantu. "Tyler Compton is missing. He should have been home nearly an hour ago."

The transportation director told Ms. Cantu that Tyler likely went to play with a neighbor. Or maybe he got off the bus at a different bus stop so he could go play with friends. That's what children do, he said. Or maybe the school failed to get the kid on the bus to begin with.

"He's five years old," said Ms. Cantu.

"Exactly," she was told.

Ms. Cantu called the Comptons again. The principal explained that the bus had returned to the bus barn and there was no sign of Tyler. Mrs. Compton burst into tears. Mr. Compton got on the phone and told Ms. Cantu that he intended to make two more phone calls: to the sheriff's office and the media.

The principal took a moment to look at the school's social media feed. Already there were many comments from the community about the missing child.

Ms. Cantu tried to think back. Surely Tyler had gotten on the bus when school ended. Most of the teachers had left the building for the day, so Ms. Cantu went to the kindergarten rooms to see if perhaps Tyler had been left behind at school.

She checked each room and then the bathrooms. No sign of Tyler. The hallways were silent.

Ms. Cantu also checked the library and the cafeteria and then headed out to the playground to look for Tyler.

When she returned to the office, her phone was ringing. The transportation director was on the other end.

"We found him!" he said. "We have Tyler, and he's fine. He's sitting in my office having a snack and some juice."

The transportation director explained that they found Tyler asleep on the bus. He had crawled under one of the seats to take a nap.

Ms. Cantu hung up immediately so she could call the Comptons. She would call the transportation department back with a few words for the director and the bus driver.

3. Issue

Five-year-old Tyler Compton did not return home from school one Thursday afternoon. The transportation department insisted that Tyler had to have gotten off the bus at his regular bus stop or perhaps another one. He had to be in his neighborhood.

According to the parents, Tyler would never go somewhere without permission. He wouldn't have gotten off the bus at another stop. The school had to know where Tyler was, and his safety was the principal's responsibility.

The transportation department also blamed the school, implying that the principal should do a much better job of supervising students getting on the bus. Obviously, the challenge could not be with the transportation department because they had policies and procedures in place to prevent problems from happening.

4. Dilemma

The transportation department in the rural school district has a policy for bus drivers to walk down the bus aisles on returning to the bus barn to check for students who might have stayed on the bus, as well as for personal items they may have been left behind.

The transportation department insisted that the five-year-old student who failed to return home after school was either still at school or playing at a friend's house. There was no way the child could have still been on the bus.

Principal Vanessa Cantu knew that the child's home was relatively far from the school, which prevented her from making a quick home visit.

The frantic parents wanted answers; they planned to call the sheriff's department and the media to help them find their child.

5. Questions

1. What previous actions has Ms. Cantu taken to make sure there would be no—or at least fewer—issues regarding bus transportation for the students? Could a principal make riding the bus routes a requirement for teachers?
2. Which steps did Ms. Cantu correctly take when she discovered that Tyler was missing? What else should she have done? What would you do differently?
3. What should Ms. Cantu tell the transportation director and the bus driver when she calls them back?
4. Should Ms. Cantu drive out to the Comptons' home to check on Tyler? Would it be better to offer to pick him up at the bus barn and drive him home?
5. Should Ms. Cantu speak with the media regarding the incident? What about posting on the social media sites her parents use?

—◦◦◦—

1. Restroom Pass

Grade Level: Urban Elementary School, Grades 3–5
Standards: 5a, b, Community of Care and Support for Students; 7b, Professional Community for Teachers and Staff; 8i, Meaningful Engagement of Families and Community

2. Background

Sunrise Elementary is an upper-elementary school consisting of grades 3 to 5. The school is located in an urban area, a bustling downtown area known for its hipster vibe. Tourists love coming to the trendy shops and restaurants in the area and enjoy hanging out and listening to music; the residents of the area are proud of their community, especially of how easily everyone embraces diversity.

The school building itself is eighty years old. Sunrise Elementary, four stories of proud red brick with keystone arch doorways and windows, sits at the corner of Bowery and South Main. There's even a small side yard for recess.

The classrooms have wooden floors, high ceilings, and large windows. The restrooms were last remodeled thirty years ago to meet the new standards of the Americans with Disabilities Act (ADA). Two stalls in every restroom were combined to make one larger area that could accommodate crutches, a walker, or a wheelchair, but little else was done to modernize or upgrade the restrooms. They still have the tall metal doors and tile walls of yesteryear.

The student population of Sunrise Elementary is ethnically diverse, and as a result, the parents and community celebrate a variety of customs to help their children understand the world around them. The demographics are 30 percent African American, 30 percent Hispanic, 20 percent white, and 20 percent Asian/Pacific Islander students. Fifty-five percent of the school is considered Title I.

The families' religions are just as diverse as their ethnicities and socioeconomic statuses: Christians, Jews, Muslims, Buddhists, and atheists are part of the school community. A few years back, there had been more than a few complaints about taking off for Christmas break between the fall and the spring semesters.

Non-Christians complained that this choice of words did not accurately describe their holiday season because they did not celebrate Christmas. These fourteen days were merely time away from school. The matter was easily resolved by changing the name of the vacation period to "Winter Break." All stakeholders seemed happy with the decision.

Another issue of possible contention occurred last year when one of the students announced that she was gender-fluid. The fifth-grade class lined up to use the restroom before lunch, and the new student, Lark, balked at using the restroom with the other girls.

She refused to go with the girls, saying, "But I'm more like a boy." Not wanting an argument in front of twenty-three other students, her teacher asked Lark to wait until all the students—boys and girls—were finished and then allowed her to use the boys' room. The rest of the students waited outside while Lark took care of her needs.

The rest of the afternoon, however, Lark's classmates teased her, saying things like, "Who do you think you are, some kind of boy?" and, "Oooh, there's a manly man in the boys' restroom!" The teacher never heard the comments or maybe simply ignored them. The teasing continued until the end of the day, and by then, Lark was nearly in tears. She refused to use either restroom before going home and, as a result, had an accident on the bus.

The teasing at this point turned to outright bullying. The students on the bus called her names and said she was a baby for soiling her clothes.

Lark's parents came to the school as soon as they discovered what had happened. They talked to both the principal and the teacher, providing background information about Lark. Lark had been sexually abused when she was much younger and, as a result, began to identify as a male to protect herself in unfamiliar settings. Lark's parents revealed the diagnosis from her psychological testing as well as the doctor's recommendations. The principal, teacher, and counselor came up with a plan to allow Lark to use the restroom of her choice.

As a follow-up, the teachers explained gender fluidity to the students in terms they could understand, and the principal sent a letter home to parents explaining gender fluidity and the school's decision to dedicate a single restroom for transgender use.

No specifics were mentioned, and the school's decision to support all children's emotional growth was largely applauded. The school's transgender bathroom policy was accepted without complaint, and several parents commended the principal for this kind of forward thinking.

Since then, Sunrise Elementary parents and the community have learned to embrace fluid gender identity. Many of the children come from same-sex parent households. In LGBT households especially, there was little pressure to conform to preset standards of gender identity. Only occasionally did some parents demand that their children use the "appropriate" bathroom.

The school administration and the teaching staff again came up with a plan for the students whose parents insisted their own children use the restroom according to anatomy rather than identity.

Sunrise Elementary now has several students who have identified as gender-fluid. In keeping with the norms of the community, the school has continued to make every effort to accommodate the emotional needs of these children. The way the school community has adopted the restroom policy and adapted it for individual children has been a topic of interest not only across the city, but also across the state. As a result, many parents of gender-fluid children want their children to go to this school.

3. Issue

As Sunrise Elementary has risen in popularity among families of gender-fluid children and advocates of recognizing diversity in the classroom, it also has come under scrutiny more often. There have been times when a policy of accommodation has proven difficult.

One such case just happened last week.

Nine-year-old Alan is in the fourth grade. Since last week, he has insisted on using the girls' restroom. He claims that he, too, is gender-fluid, just like another boy in his class.

Because gender fluidity has been so openly accepted in the school, the teacher allowed Alan to select the restroom pass he preferred. He took the girls' pass, and the teacher didn't think anything of it.

Alan was out of the classroom for fifteen minutes. When the teacher asked what took so long, he shrugged his shoulders and said, "I had to go." The class laughed, and the teacher didn't think about it again.

Each day for a week, Alan made trips to the girls' restroom. Each trip was longer than the last.

As the new week began, several parents waited for the principal. The parents had one thing in common: they had a daughter in the fourth grade, and that daughter reported that someone was in the restroom "watching" them last week. Every girl named Alan as the watcher.

Each girl reported her story, and it quickly became apparent that Alan was more than just a voyeur; he was perhaps an assailant.

4. Dilemma

One fourth-grade male student, Alan, has abused the schools' gender-fluid policy regarding restroom use to spy on girls using the restroom; it is possible that he also assaulted them. Alan gained access to the girls' restroom by claiming that he was gender-fluid.

His prolonged absences from the classroom give Alan no alibi; it was the girls' words against his. His teacher remembers only that he was gone "for a while."

The parents of the fourth-grade girls are demanding that something be done about Alan; they want to press charges against him. They also want the transgender bathroom policy stopped immediately.

5. Questions

1. How did the transgender bathroom policy at Sunrise Elementary help gender-fluid students? Why is this important?
2. What is the Sunrise Elementary restroom policy regarding transgender students? How did Alan violate that policy? Why is this important?
3. What steps should Alan's teacher have taken last week when Alan wanted to use the girls' restroom? What other strategies could the teacher implement regarding restroom use?
4. Should Sunrise Elementary change their transgender restroom policy or get rid of it altogether? Why or why not?
5. Can the parents press charges against Alan? If they can, should they? Why or why not?
6. How can the principal speak up as an advocate for all students? If you were the principal and had one to two minutes to make an appeal on behalf of your students, what would you say?

1. The Red Sweater

Grade Level: Urban Elementary School, Grades PK–5
Standards: 5a, b, Community of Care and Support for Students

2. Background

Sarah B. Jones hated four things, and she hated them all equally: school, Billy Buford, her red sweater, and Brussels sprouts.

Fortunately, the school cafeteria never served Brussels sprouts. Unfortunately, however, Sarah's mother made her wear the dreaded red sweater to school every day. Every time Sarah wore the sweater, Billy teased her about it. "Shred the red," he croaked when Sarah walked by. "Red's got no cred."

The jeers made Sarah hate her sweater all the more. It was a hand-me-down from her older sisters. Each one of them had worn the red sweater to school, and now it was Sarah's turn. The fabric had been patched a couple of times, and the buttons had been replaced so many times that they didn't match. Sarah was embarrassed that she had only this one outer garment to wear when it was chilly.

Sometimes Sarah purposefully left her sweater in the room when the class went to recess. It meant being cold, but Sarah didn't care. She didn't want to be bullied anymore. Better to be freezing to death than to be made fun of, Sarah thought.

"What's wrong you, Sarah?" asked her teacher, Mrs. Grouse. "Everybody else has enough sense to wear a jacket or a sweater when it's cold outside. Everybody but you."

The rest of the class laughed. Billy made a gesture that looked like he was trying to throw up. Sarah wanted to disappear. Mrs. Grouse didn't see him make the gesture. She also didn't hear when he began whispering, "No sense Sarah."

Sarah's eyes filled with tears, and she put her head down on her desk.

"And no sleeping in my class," said Mrs. Grouse. "That's why you're behind in your schoolwork."

Sarah mumbled something about having to go to the restroom and left the room. She took her sweater with her.

She was gone for a long time. The only person who seemed to notice was Frank, the day custodian. He was in the hallway when Sarah came out of the girls' restroom and walked slowly back to her classroom.

"That poor girl," Frank thought. "Dressed in thin clothes and no sweater, no jacket, no nothing." He made a mental note to look for something nice left in the lost-and-found long ago. He'd have his wife wash it up real nice for Sarah.

It wasn't until much later in the day that Frank made the connection between Sarah's lack of warm clothing and her restroom visit. Around two o'clock, one of the teachers reported that there was water all over the floor near the girls' restroom.

Frank discovered the culprit: an overflowing toilet. Clear water ran up over the sides of the bowl and splashed onto the floor. If he hadn't known better, he would think something was clogging the valve and keeping it open. Surely not, he thought. Then he realized what had happened. He went to get the principal, Chris Conway.

The principal happened to be in her office.

"Come on in, Frank," she said. "You look like you have something on your mind."

"Oh, I do," he said. "But I think you need to come see this for yourself."

Frank took Ms. Conway to the restroom. He directed her to stand back just a bit while he inserted a coat hanger with a hook at one end into the toilet. Sure enough, he snagged something right way and pulled. Soon he had pulled enough at the object so that they could both see a red sleeve.

Frank pulled the rest of the sweater out of the toilet.

"Do you know who did this?" asked Ms. Conway.

"Yes, I believe I do," he said, putting the soggy wet sweater in a clear plastic trash bag. He filled the principal in on his suspicions.

"Frank, please take the bag and put it on my desk," said Ms. Conway. "I'll be there shortly."

Ms. Conway went to Sarah's classroom and paused before turning the doorknob. She could hear Mrs. Grouse shouting from the other side of the door. Ms. Conway stepped inside, saying, "Good news everyone! Mrs. Grouse has agreed to let me read you a story today. I just happened to have some time right now while your teacher takes a fifteen-minute break." She motioned for Mrs. Grouse to leave the room.

Ms. Conway selected a book and read it to the students. She noticed Billy making faces at Sarah. When she was finished reading and Mrs. Grouse had returned, the principal said, "Sarah, would you mind helping me for a bit in my office? I'm sure Mrs. Grouse won't mind."

Sarah smiled and took her principal's hand. Together they walked out of the classroom and toward the office.

"Sarah, I think you may have been going through some difficult times," said Ms. Conway. "Would you care to talk about them?"

Sarah saw the red sweater sitting on the principal's desk, and she began to cry.

3. Issue

Sarah has been the victim of bullying in her classroom because of a second-hand sweater she has to wear. She is embarrassed to be seen in it. Not only has one student in particular bullied, but also the teacher has been cruel by making comments based on generalizations.

As a result, Sarah doesn't like school, and she is disengaged from her academic work. She often tries to leave the sweater behind, hoping that it won't be discovered, even if not wearing the sweater means being cold.

To get rid of the sweater, Sarah has flushed it down one of the toilets in the girls' restroom.

4. Dilemma

Frank, the custodian, told Principal Chris Conway his suspicions about Sarah. He had seen Sarah earlier, walking slowly back to her classroom. It was almost as though she didn't want to be there.

As Frank walked past the room, he heard the teacher yelling, "And where do you think you've been, with this much time gone by?" He knew that Mrs. Grouse yelled frequently and loudly in her classroom. Sometimes he could hear her from the end of the hall.

Frank informed the principal of his concern for Sarah. When Principal Conway went to the classroom door, she heard Mrs. Grouse yelling at the children, so she asked the teacher to take a break while she read a story.

In the classroom, she saw Billy Buford make nasty faces at Sarah but didn't say anything. She invited Sarah to her office so she could find out what was really going on.

5. Questions

1. Is Sarah in trouble for plugging up the toilet? Should she be?
2. Did the principal do the right thing in asking the teacher to take a break from the class? What would you have done differently?
3. What should the principal do about Mrs. Grouse?
4. What consequences, if any, should Billy receive? Explain your answer.
5. What should Ms. Conway's next steps be? Who should be involved in helping Sarah with the bullying in her classroom?

1. The Field Trip

Grade Level: Urban Elementary School, Grades K–5
Standards: 5a, Community of Care and Support for Students; 8b, c, Meaningful Engagement of Families and Community

2. Background

Mr. Holleman, principal of West Elementary, grabbed his cup of coffee and headed to the first grade-level meeting of the day. He would be meeting with one of his favorite teams of teachers, the second-grade team.

The second-grade teachers—all seven of them—were a joy to work with because they knew how to prepare quality lessons from the district curriculum. They also worked as a model team, one that any principal would love to have on campus. One day a week, they met outside the school day, not because they had to, but because they wanted to.

It was their mutually agreed-upon way to make sure they were all on the same page and had every activity prepared for the week. That meant ensuring diversity in activities for not only their gifted and talented students but also their English-language-learner (ELL) population and their special-education students.

When they had first begun their practice of once-a-week meetings outside the school day, Mr. Holleman's phone rang just after 6:00 a.m. It was the lead cafeteria lady. She wanted to know why he was requiring teachers to report to work so early. He had never made this a mandate; the teachers came up with this on their own. As a result, they got a lot of work done, and they produced stellar results. In return, Mr. Holleman tried to make sure he kept these teachers happy.

Mr. Holleman stood at the door of the conference room, greeting the teachers as they came in. They were all in an exceptionally good mood, he noted. That was a good thing because he needed to ask for their help in planning a parent meeting regarding student behavior. Several of the second-graders had been sent to his office for poor behavior, and some of the parents of other students had begun complaining.

The school had just begun a new discipline approach aimed at recognizing students for their positive behaviors. Some of the students were still having challenges conforming to the school's—and their teachers'—expectations. It was time to get a handle on the situation before things got really bad.

The second-grade teachers had agenda items to discuss as well, and it looked as though they had brought materials with them. Mr. Holleman noticed a particularly thick folder.

"Ladies . . . and gentleman," Mr. Holleman said, with a nod to the only male teacher, Mr. Garcia, "you'll see from the first agenda item that we'll be discussing student behavior today. I know there have been some, er, challenging students in second grade this year, and I'd like us to work with the parents on solving some of our discipline problems. Maybe the parents can also offer some insight on how the new behavior system is working out."

"Some of the parents are the challenge," muttered one of the teachers.

"Oh, yes," said Mrs. Davis, the second-grade lead teacher. "We've had our hands quite full this year. In fact, our positive rewards system seems to work for some of the students but not all of them." She peered over her bifocals and squinted. "I think you know who I'm talking about."

"Yeah, there are about fifteen of them, but I'd say three or four are the absolute worst," added Ms. Johnson. "I'd love to see parents at a meeting about discipline and behavior, but the ones we really need to talk to are the ones who won't come to the meeting."

Mr. Holleman brought everyone back into focus on the idea of having a parent meeting to discuss student behavior and review the school's current positive-behavior support plan. The agenda would include a review of the behavior-management system, and the teachers would involve parents in determining goals and rewards that could be earned.

"Okay, what's on your agenda?" Mr. Holleman asked, pointing to the folder the teachers had carried in.

"Well, as you know, we are just about to complete our unit on wild versus domestic animals," said Mr. Garcia. "We'd like to conclude with an educational field trip to the zoo. It ties in with our instruction over the last six weeks."

"We have everything right here," said Mrs. Davis as she pushed the big folder toward Mr. Holleman. The rest of the teachers beamed. They obviously worked hard on the contents.

"So who is going on this trip?" Mr. Holleman asked.

"Everyone," said Mrs. Link, motioning to the teachers seated at the table. "We'd also like to borrow some of the instructional assistants from pre-kindergarten and kindergarten to help us out."

Mr. Holleman looked through the contents of the folder. There was an itinerary, a budget breakdown, and lesson plans showing learning objectives for the field trip, as well as how these activities connected to pre- and post-activities done in the classroom. The activities had a considerable amount of differentiation so that students at all levels could participate successfully in learning.

There was a field trip participation form that contained a request for current contact information in case of an emergency, a list of instructional assistants the teachers wanted to have on the trip, and a single page listing the students with health concerns such as allergies to peanuts and insect stings.

It seemed as though this instructional team had thought of everything. Then Mr. Holleman noticed another piece of paper listing the names of fifteen students.

"What's this?" he asked as he read the names on the list. As the principal, he knew every one of these students very well.

"It's a list of students who are not going," said Mrs. Davis.

Mr. Holleman raised an eyebrow. "Not going?"

"Obviously these kids cannot go on the trip," said Mrs. Davis. "They are our biggest troublemakers. We can't take them with us."

Mr. Holleman looked at the names again. Eight of the fifteen were special-education students, and of those eight three were on behavior plans. Four more students were identified as 504-plan students; they took medication during the school day for ADHD.

One student was a known "runner" who took off randomly during instructional time, running away from the adults who supervised him. Mr. Holleman knew the parents of these students well, and he knew that they would be unlikely to tolerate their children missing out on a great opportunity like this field trip.

The principal asked which teacher would be staying with the students who did not go on the trip.

The team members looked at each other. They said they would place the students in other classrooms so that all the second-grade teachers could go on the field trip together.

3. Issue

Principal Holleman has called a parent meeting at West Elementary for the parents of second-graders. He is aware that the current behavior program is not working as well as it should be, and he wants to explore possible revisions for the positive-behavior support program and gather suggestions for program changes if necessary.

The second-grade teachers want to take the entire grade level on an instructional field trip to the zoo. However, they have also provided the principal a list of students who cannot go due to poor behavior. Many of these students are in special education, and several, according to their IEPs, have behavior plans. Preventing them from going could be a violation of the IEPs.

4. Dilemma

Eight of the fifteen students on the list to miss the field trip are in special education, and more than one-third of them are on behavior plans. Several more students have qualified for 504 services because of their ADHD. Taking the students on the field trip will mean a considerable amount of work, especially because of the behavior challenges. One of the students often tries to run away from the teachers and hide.

The teachers are concerned about student safety, but they also want to deny student attendance due to bad behavior. Leaving the students with behavior problems behind means that they may act up in another teacher's classroom. Also, students might not receive their minutes of service as set forth in the IEPs.

5. Questions

1. Should the administration go ahead and hold the parent meeting about behavior? What should the meeting agenda consist of?
2. Can the administration and teachers talk about the behaviors of specific students during the parent meeting? What about the medications some students are taking? What should the school employees do if other parents bring it up? What other options, besides a parent meeting, exist?
3. What, if anything, should Mr. Holleman tell the teachers about their choice to leave students with behavior issues behind?
4. How can the teachers and administration plan for enough supervision if every student goes on the field trip?
5. Should Mr. Holleman approve the second-grade field trip? Why or why not?

Chapter Four

Human Resource Management

―☙―

1. Social Media Mavens

Grade Level: Urban Elementary Charter School, Grades K–5
Standards: 6a, b, Professional Capacity of School Personnel

2. Background

Every year, Spring Charter Elementary saw about a 30 percent turnover in staff. The school was located downtown in an area riddled with crime. The building was an old storefront located in what had been a small but trendy strip mall and now was the charter elementary campus and central-office administration building.

To suggest there was a central-office administration was misleading. Central office consisted of the superintendent and a secretary who also served as the elementary campus's registrar.

The principal, Wendy McClure, was in charge of curriculum, special education, and state assessment in addition to the rest of her duties as principal. The work was hard, but she loved it, largely because the charter freed her from some of the bureaucracy found in a more traditional school district. In addition, she felt as though she was making a difference in the lives of kids who needed help the most.

The population of Spring Elementary was 60 percent African American, 30 percent Hispanic, and 10 percent white. The school was a Title I school due to the economically disadvantaged population.

Finding teachers to work with this population was difficult. Teachers had to understand that their students most likely weren't going to be on grade level when they first enrolled at Spring. Getting them caught up took a lot of extra time, and many of the teachers tutored after school and on weekends.

Absenteeism was high among students and teachers.

The superintendent often reminded Ms. McClure that charter schools were not required to hire teachers with professional teaching certificates, but Ms. McClure felt that her students deserved services as good as, if not better than, those in the traditional district.

She fought to hire certified teachers, and sometimes the school year was close to starting before she could get all of her faculty onboard.

The other problem was that the charter district did not offer contracts. Teachers could quit whenever they wanted, and although the district requested thirty days' notice, they were often lucky if they got three days' notice. Novice teachers accepted employment with Spring but then continued their search for a better teaching job. When they found it, they left.

It was no wonder that when Ms. McClure interviewed the Adams sisters during the second week of August, she was excited. The young African American women were twins, and they had both majored in education, obtaining degrees and certification in elementary education. They were looking for a place to work where they would be together and have benefits, like insurance, as well. They loved kids and were eager to work with them.

Ms. McClure explained the workload, and the two young women thought they could handle it. They could help each other, especially if they were going to be in the same grade level.

Ms. McClure hired them on the spot. School would start next week.

The Adams twins wanted to set up their classrooms right away and get the books they would need. Ms. McClure was pleased with their enthusiasm and gave them what they needed.

The high levels of energy continued through the first grading period. By the time progress report grades were due, in the second grading period, Ms. McClure noticed they had a little less energy for teaching. When the third six weeks began, neither Adams sister wanted to stay after school to tutor, and they begged off working on weekends.

More than once, Ms. McClure noticed that they, especially Amanda, nodded off in the classroom. She pulled Amanda aside to ask what was going on.

"I'm tired, that's all," said Amanda. "So is Alison. We both had to take second jobs to help pay off our student loans."

"Hmmm, are you aware that you could get loan assistance because of the at-risk population you work with? Let me get you the paperwork on that—it could help."

"Um, yeah, sure," said Amanda.

For a while, the twins performed a little better in the classroom, but then their work began to slip again.

"I'm worried about those two," said Ms. McClure. "I really want to find a way to help them."

The secretary/registrar turned and looked at the principal. "I don't think the money is their issue," she said.

"What do you mean?" asked Ms. McClure.

"Apparently they're making money hand over fist, or maybe I should say hand over thong, and they've been doing it for years," said the secretary/registrar. "Haven't you seen what the parents are talking about on social media? Look here."

The secretary/registrar thumbed on her phone over to a page of pictures and videos. There were the Adams twins, pole-dancing together in a strip club, wearing nothing but high heels and thongs. Their performance had garnered hundreds of comments, many from parents whose names the principal recognized.

To make matters worse, Alison and Amanda responded to the parents' comments, often making lewd comments and inviting them to the club.

Ms. McClure called the teachers to her office at the end of the day.

"We can't stay, ma'am," said Alison. "We have to be at our other job."

"I know all about it," said Ms. McClure, "and we need to talk."

3. Issue

Ms. McClure has difficulty finding and retaining highly qualified teachers to work at Spring Charter Elementary School. When she does find them, they don't stay long, looking for better pay and working conditions.

When she hires two sisters for teaching positions, their second job is one that pairs poorly with teaching. They work as strippers at night.

Many pictures and videos of the two of them are beginning to surface on social media. Not only are the parents making comments, but the teachers are engaging in discussion with them.

4. Dilemma

Ms. McClure is always on the lookout for highly qualified teachers. She found two by hiring the Adams sisters. Now that she has discovered what they do at their second jobs, she needs to decide if she should keep them on the faculty or let them go

5. Questions

1. What are some things Ms. McClure could have done to look into Alison's and Amanda's backgrounds before hiring them?
2. What initiatives could Ms. McClure put into place to lighten the teachers' workloads?
3. Should Ms. McClure fire the Adams sisters on the spot? Why or why not?
4. Whether the Adams sisters quit or are fired, what can Ms. McClure do to fill the position, either temporarily or permanently?
5. What incentive plans could the principal and superintendent put into place to retain teachers not only throughout the year but in the following years?

—◦/◦/◦—

1. Custodial Calamity

Grade Level: Rural Elementary School, Grades PK–5
Standards: 6b, c, h, i, Professional Capacity of School Personnel

2. Background

Ducindra Connor had been the head custodian at Rock Springs Elementary for the last twelve years. She had been a valued part of the staff, eager to take care of the building and supervise a custodial team of three other members.

Ms. Connor's duties at this rural school included creating schedules for the custodial staff, assigning duties and cleaning areas, evaluating the job performance of her team, and attending maintenance and facilities department meetings.

The meetings were a particular favorite of Ms. Connor's because they were held off-site at the central office building. They often lasted six hours, and that was six hours that Ms. Connor didn't have to dust, mop, or clean up muddy footprints and occasional vomit. It was six hours of bliss, as far as she was concerned. It was also an opportunity to form relationships with other head custodians and managers in the custodial department.

One day, Ms. Connor thought, she would like nothing more than to work at central office, have a great big desk in her own office, and help with supervising the cleaning care of all of the schools in the district.

That's why whenever central office held a meeting for all of the head custodians in the district, Ms. Connor always made her special banana bread and a few other treats to share with everyone in the meeting. Her presence was much anticipated because of her baked goods and the stories she told about her experiences in custodial management. She knew especially well how to save money and get her work done under budget, and she was also the superintendent's cousin.

When the school board approved hiring Principal Jake Johnson to replace the retiring principal of Rock Springs Elementary, most of the staff at the school was happy that they were getting a new administrator. The former principal had become complacent, and as long as no one rocked the boat, he allowed several of the teachers and other staff members to do very little work. This was especially true of the head custodian. The former principal had hired Ms. Connor, based on the superintendent's recommendation.

At first, Ms. Connor's work was outstanding. She was energetic and eager to do a great job. She was able to quickly clean her areas of the school and she still found time to take on extra projects for maintenance. As the years went by, however, Ms. Connor's work quality began to slip. She often cut corners, skipped cleaning some parts of the school, and assigned herself the easier shifts each week.

By the time the new principal, Jake Johnson, moved into his office, Ms. Connor had been allowed to do whatever she wanted. All of that was about to change.

Mr. Johnson finished unpacking the few items he brought with him, turned around, and wrinkled his nose. "What's that smell?" he asked.

His secretary said, "I'm not sure what you're talking about."

Mr. Johnson thought for a moment. Surely the smell hadn't come in with the boxes. He inhaled deeply again. "That smell," he said. "It's musty and old, almost like something has spoiled."

The secretary insisted she couldn't smell it.

As Mr. Johnson became acclimated to the school, he visited all of the areas in the building. That included classrooms, restrooms, the gym, the library, and even the book rooms. Everywhere he went, he noticed the same smell.

Finally, he visited the custodial room where the cleaning supplies, district documents, and tools were stored. The smell that he had noticed everywhere else was especially strong in this room.

"Hey, what's this?" he asked, as he pointed to a mop bucket full of dirty water.

"That's my mop water," said Ms. Connor.

"Wow, I had no idea the school floors could get that dirty in a day," said Mr. Johnson.

"Oh that's not just for one day," said Ms. Connor. "That's a week's worth of mopping."

Mr. Johnson raised an eyebrow. "A week's worth?"

"Sure. Once I mix the water and the cleaner, I use it all week. It's easier and we go through less cleaner. That saves money and time."

"From now on, Ms. Connor, I'd like you to change that mop water every day. This school has a very musty smell to it, and I think it's because you're mopping with dirty water."

She looked at Mr. Johnson squarely and said, "You can't tell me what to do because I'm related to the superintendent."

"I can and will tell you what to do because I'm the principal. My directive to you is to change the mop water daily," said Mr. Johnson.

Mr. Johnson left the custodial room and went back to his office.

Within the hour, he got a call at his desk. Ms. Connor was on the other end, telling him that she was leaving the campus because she had fallen and hurt her ankle when she was changing the mop water. She was headed to the doctor to get her ankle x-rayed.

The next day Mr. Johnson received the doctor's report. Ms. Connor had broken her ankle and was unable to come to work for the next three months. Because she had been a full-time employee, she was eligible for time off under the Family and Medical Leave Act (FMLA).

With his head custodian at home recuperating, Mr. Johnson needed to select a temporary one. He met with each and every member of the custodial team and selected a new hire by the name of Todd Ragdale.

Mr. Ragdale took over Ms. Connor's duties with zealousness. He wanted to prove that he could do a great job. He made several changes immediately, including reassigning duties and changing the mop water several times a day. Mr. Ragdale made sure, during the next three months, that he scheduled himself for a variety of shifts, not taking the best ones for himself but showing his team that he was willing to work side by side with them. In three short months, he got the school in tip-top shape, and the teachers and parents noticed it.

Everyone was pleased with the changes.

3. Issue

At the end of three months, it was time for Ms. Connor to come back to work. Mr. Ragdale was disappointed that his former boss was supposed to return, and the teachers felt that the new changes would be lost.

So did Mr. Johnson.

On Monday when Ms. Connor was supposed to return to work from her FMLA absence, she did not show up. Mr. Johnson phoned her; there was no answer, so he left a voice-mail for her to return his call.

In the meantime, Mr. Johnson received a complaint from one of the other custodians who had been at the school for several years and was good friends with Ms. Connor. Mr. Ragdale had redecorated the custodial room, she said, and she felt that she couldn't work for him. She didn't even think she could go in the custodial room anymore to get her supplies because of the calendars and posters of scantily dressed females all over the walls.

4. Dilemma

Ms. Connor's extended leave created an opportunity for a new head custodian to temporarily step in and take on the duties of cleaning and caring for the school building. Her replacement, Mr. Ragdale, had been doing an excellent job, and the people in the building really appreciated everything he had been doing. Mr. Johnson, the principal, was exceptionally pleased.

Upon receiving the complaint from one of the custodial team members, Mr. Johnson went immediately to the custodial room to see how Mr. Ragdale had redecorated it. The walls held several large posters of voluptuous women in barely-there garments. The calendar sitting open on Mr. Ragdale's small desk revealed similarly clad women sprawled across cars.

Mr. Ragdale walked in behind Mr. Johnson. "Yeah, I spruced things up in here, too. Looks good, right?"

5. Questions

1. What should Mr. Johnson's response be to Mr. Ragdale's posters and the calendar? Why?
2. Should Mr. Johnson have addressed Ms. Connor's response to him about the mop water, and if so, how?
3. What should Mr. Johnson do about Ms. Connor not showing up for work after her FMLA absence period ended? Look up FMLA, and get the exact language that would be referenced when communicating with Ms. Connor.
4. Which custodian is more fit for the job? Why?
5. What would you recommend to Mr. Johnson regarding finding a permanent head custodian? Explain your answer.
6. Who else should be involved in the decision making and why?

1. Time for Professional Development

Grade Level: Urban Elementary School, Grades PK–5
Standards: 6g, h, i, Professional Capacity of School Personnel

2. Background

Jenny Wyatt had been a principal for more years than many of her teachers had been teaching.

Mrs. Wyatt was an excellent principal who involved the community and parents in her students' instruction, saw that the students were treated equitably, and doted on her teachers as much as she did the children who attended T. Clifford Elementary.

Together, she and the faculty came up with the motto, "Education at Clifford suits me to a T." She was sure the school's namesake, Theodore Clifford, or "T" as he preferred to be called, would have loved that.

There was a lot to love both about Mrs. Wyatt's campus and about her.

This principal maintained an elaborate master list of all of her teachers and their professional development goals and needs, and she updated that list frequently. Their growth as educators was important to her. Mrs. Wyatt wanted to have the best-trained staff anywhere, and she orchestrated a variety of strategies to make sure they had cutting-edge information.

Principal Wyatt liked to begin the year with a motivational speaker who would inspire and energize the teachers in preparing for the work ahead. She also included time for district leaders to share their knowledge about new initiatives. Mrs. Wyatt avidly searched the training available through the local education service center to augment the training needs for her teachers.

Regular dialogue about student progress was always part of the picture. Mrs. Wyatt discussed student needs with her teachers at grade-level meetings, during site-based decision-making sessions, and individually.

She met with her teachers informally and individually every six weeks for a discussion about how things were going in their classrooms. She used coaching techniques she had learned years ago, and she asked open-ended questions about the teachers' successes and roadblocks for that grading period. She also wanted to know if they felt that they had adequate training for what they needed to do. Mrs. Wyatt always concluded every conversation with two questions:

• What do you need for your students to be successful in the next six weeks?
• How can I help you with that?

The teachers were not afraid to ask for whatever they needed. "It's almost like going to Mom for a little help," they would say. "She's always there for us."

Mrs. Wyatt was like a mom to many of the teachers because she was always available. Whenever the principal had an idea for one of the teachers, she called right away to discuss it.

"Megan, I had a thought," Mrs. Wyatt would begin. "I think you should present at the state conference next semester, and I want you to put a proposal together for it. Tell me what you need, and I'll help."

The problem was that Mrs. Wyatt made these calls without regard to time of day. She was just as likely to call at eleven at night as at five in the morning. If she was awake, she was fairly certain her teachers were awake, too.

"Just like a mom," the teachers would laugh. No one had the courage to ask Mrs. Wyatt to observe more realistic times when calling after hours. They knew she would always be there.

That was the other problem. Mrs. Wyatt was always there at the campus. She never took a sick day, and she never took a professional-development day. Her attendance was outstanding. It always had been and likely always would be. She was off campus for only a few hours at a time for leadership meetings with the other principals in the district.

"The campus needs its principal every day," said Mrs. Wyatt. "Besides, Clifford suits me to a T."

Clifford Elementary practically ran itself, thanks to the systems Mrs. Wyatt had put into place over the years. In the beginning, she put in fourteen- and sixteen-hour days, but now she tried to work no more than ten hours a day. Every campus employee knew what to do, and they did it because it was the right thing to do. Professionalism mattered to the teachers and staff alike.

As much as Mrs. Wyatt supported professional development for her teachers, she all but refused it for herself. "It's hard to teach an old gal like me new tricks," she told her colleagues. "I feel like I've seen it all."

Mrs. Wyatt did seem to know quite a few of the education-thought leaders of the time. She had their books, but she also had their phone numbers and would call them if one of her teachers needed help.

She didn't seek out her own professional development, and she wasn't interested in presenting at conferences, either.

"Oh, honey, people don't care about what I have to say. There are lots of other people who can say it lots better," Mrs. Wyatt told her teachers and peers whenever they asked about her sharing what she learned over the years. "Besides, there's such new stuff out there today. It's the younger teachers' turn to go meet people and make connections."

Mrs. Wyatt's preference was to stay at the campus and work. In fact, work mattered to her the most.

"And I can always call one of my teachers if I have a question."

3. Issue

Principal Jenny Wyatt wants the best for her teachers, and she sees to it that they get whatever they need to teach the students at Clifford Elementary.

Mrs. Wyatt is especially keen on getting her teachers the best professional development possible. She plans for campus-wide training as well as individual opportunities for each teacher. Mrs. Wyatt relies on coaching strategies to elicit honest answers and problem-solving strategies from her teachers.

She feels as though she is familiar enough with her staff to call them at any time to discuss school matters. She calls very late at night, when most people have gone to bed, or very early in the morning, when people are either still asleep or trying to get their day started.

Mrs. Wyatt refuses to attend professional development for herself.

4. Dilemma

Principal Jenny Wyatt has become complacent about her own professional development, choosing to stay on the campus to work rather than continue learning anything new in the education field or sharing her vast knowledge.

She doesn't read in her field or engage in any other training because she feels she's already seen it all. The only thing she will attend off campus is district-mandated leadership meetings.

In addition, Mrs. Wyatt has become like a mom to many of her teachers, looking out for them and meeting with them individually to help them identify and reach their goals. The problem, though, is that Mrs. Wyatt will call them extremely late at night or early in the morning to talk about ideas.

No teacher has been brave enough to ask Mrs. Wyatt to stop calling at unreasonable times.

5. Questions

1. What does Mrs. Wyatt do well for her teachers?
2. What's the problem with Mrs. Wyatt calling her teachers after hours? Is there a time that is too late or too early to call?
3. What are appropriate reasons to call a teacher after the school day is over?
4. Do you agree or disagree that eventually a principal will have "seen it all" in regard to professional development? Why or why not?
5. If you were one of the principals in the leadership meetings with Mrs. Wyatt, what would you recommend to her regarding professional development?

1. Legendary Lothario

Grade Level: Suburban Elementary School, Grades K–5
Standards: 7c, e, Professional Community for Teachers and Staff

2. Background

Logan Keith wanted more than anything to be the principal at Earhart Elementary. He had been an assistant principal for six years, and now he felt he was ready to lead a team of teachers. After all, he had certainly done harder jobs.

Before becoming a teacher himself and then an administrator, Mr. Keith had worked in construction, but he never really quit the building industry. He accepted side projects during holidays and some of the longer breaks in the school year. According to Mr. Keith, it was a good way to stay fit while earning a little extra cash.

Maybe when he was the principal, he wouldn't keep his second job. He could give up construction for good.

The current principal of Earhart Elementary was retiring, finally. Mr. Keith thought she'd never make up her mind and decide to enjoy her golden years. Mr. Keith applied for her job as soon as it was posted. Poised to take over the reins of the campus, Mr. Keith looked forward to the meeting at which the school board would announce their decision to replace the retiring principal with him.

The next day, Mr. Keith didn't want to go to work. He had not been appointed principal. The new principal of Earhart Elementary would be someone with only two years' experience as an assistant principal. She had acquired most of her teaching experience in the secondary grades, and her only two years in administration were spent on an elementary campus. She wasn't even from the area, like Mr. Keith was.

Amy Black, the new principal, arrived at the campus with the superintendent, who wanted to introduce the new principal to the faculty and staff. Mrs. Black seemed nice enough, and Mr. Keith admitted, she had some pretty good ideas about how to help the teachers with instruction. Too bad she was married, he thought. She was pretty, too.

As they left the meeting, Amy Black assured the superintendent she was up to the challenge of taking on this elementary as its principal. The superintendent cautioned her that not everyone would be an ally in making the changes needed at this campus, and if she noticed anything suspicious, she was to enlist the support of human resources immediately.

Mrs. Black thought the superintendent's remarks were odd, considering that she had stressed that academic improvement was the number-one priority for Earhart Elementary. Its state assessment scores trailed behind all of the other elementary campuses in the district. The school needed an immediate turnaround, and that's why Mrs. Black was here.

First, though, Mrs. Black wanted to meet with her team. She set up meeting times to talk with everyone, from teachers to custodians, the office staff, and parents. She also wanted to meet with Mr. Keith Keith to get his perspective on the campus's strengths and weaknesses.

When Mrs. Black met with Mr. Keith, she was direct, asking if he thought he would be able to work for her since he had applied for this position and been turned down.

"Yes, I think I can," Mr. Keith said. "You have some fresh new ideas, and I think they will help the campus."

"Good," said Mrs. Black. "I'm counting on your 100-percent effort to help make this a great year for the students at Earhart."

"You have my support," said Mr. Keith. "There is one thing, though. I would like to supervise the instructional assistants. I was once an assistant and I think I can be a good mentor to them."

"Okay," said Mrs. Black.

When Mrs. Black met with her campus secretary, Mrs. Smith, the woman advised her, "Be careful with that one." She nodded in the direction of Logan Keith's office. "He's quite the lothario, if you know what I mean."

"I don't know what you mean," said Mrs. Black.

"Watch him with the women on campus. You'll see," said Mrs. Smith cryptically.

Mrs. Black didn't think about the comments again until the first day of school.

Everyone arrived early to make sure the day began smoothly for the parents and their children. When Mrs. Black walked into the office area, she noticed that the registrar and attendance clerk had a single long-stemmed red rose on their desks. Mrs. Smith's rose was sticking up out of her trashcan.

There was no rose on Mrs. Black's desk. That seemed odd, but she tried to ignore it.

"Wow, who brought roses?" Mrs. Black asked of no one in particular.

"Mr. Keith. He does it all the time," said Mrs. Smith.

Mrs. Black felt that it was fine to hand out roses as long as everyone received one. Giving teachers roses on the first day of instruction was a nice gesture, one she was sure they appreciated. She wondered if the male teachers got them, too.

Next, Mrs. Black began to visit the teachers' classrooms to say good morning. As she went from room to room, she noticed that not all of the teachers or even all of the instructional assistants had received flowers. Only the younger, prettier women had received them.

Mrs. Black observed Mr. Keith throughout the day. He frequently visited the classrooms, where he had left roses, especially one where an unmarried instructional assistant named Miss Jackson had been assigned. At lunchtime, he assisted her with escorting the students to the cafeteria. By the end of the day, the two employees stood extremely close to each other in private conversation.

The next day, Mr. Keith asked if Mrs. Black would mind him taking his lunch off campus. Miss Jackson needed to get a couple of errands run, and he wanted to accompany her.

3. Issue

Assistant Principal Logan Keith wanted to be the principal of Earhart Elementary, but Amy Black was appointed as the replacement for the retiring principal. The assistant principal was not selected to lead the campus, and, in fact, the superintendent has suspicions about his behavior. She would not reveal what these suspicions are.

Mr. Keith is a ladies' man, and on the first day of school he presented the youngest and prettiest women on the campus with roses. He frequently favored the young women on campus, and he insisted on being their supervisor so he could help them grow in their careers.

4. Dilemma

Assistant Principal Logan Keith wants to take one of the instructional assistants he supervises out during lunch to get her errands run. Just the day before, they were seen having a private conversation while standing closely together. In addition, Mr. Keith often presents the youngest and most beautiful women on campus with long-stemmed roses.

Mr. Keith has asked for permission from principal Amy Black to leave the campus during the lunch period with the instructional assistant.

5. Questions

1. Should Mrs. Black allow Mr. Keith to take the instructional assistant off campus to run errands? Why or why not?
2. What behavior has the assistant principal exhibited that may seem questionable?
3. Should the superintendent have been more specific in telling Principal Amy Black what to look for in Mr. Keith's behavior?
4. Why did Mrs. Smith receive a rose?
5. What other school leadership standard does this case study involve? Why is this important to understand in this context?

———◌/◌/◌———

1. Playing Possum

Grade Level: Rural Elementary School, Grades PK–5
Standards: 9c, d, Operations and Management

2. Background

Jeff Smith is the principal at Possum Valley Elementary, a rural school that educates approximately four hundred students. Buses travel the expansive district, bringing students to the campus from considerable distances.

Possum Valley attracts quite a few families to the area from bigger cities in the state. People who move there from urban areas are usually looking for a less stressful, more laid-back way of life. They have been able to make the transition from city life to country life thanks to telecommuting. These parents want a wholesome community in which to raise their kids. With its abundance of small-town charm and wildlife, Possum Valley offers all that and more.

As a result of this migration, several subdivisions have sprung up around the small township. Families can find affordable homes on large lots, and they have come to appreciate the deer, raccoons, and other wild animals that wander across their yards.

Other students come from the nearby farms; they've grown up in the country. They know how to fish and hunt and have considerable knowledge of the plants and wildlife where they live.

Other students are from families who live in low-income housing and barely scrape by each month.

Many of the students who come from the farms nap or do their homework on the buses because the commute can be almost an hour in some cases. The roads are rural routes that wind past the farms and their vast fields of crops. When they get home, the children often help with a few chores around the farm, have supper, and turn in for the night.

On weekends, the children from Possum Valley get together to play organized T-ball, softball, and soccer at the district's baseball and soccer fields. Sometimes the community uses the high school track. Often the teachers and Mr. Smith himself will join in these leisure activities. The elementary campus traditionally has two festivals a year, one in the fall and one in the summer, to raise money for the student activity fund.

Possum Valley Elementary is one of the older campuses in the school district. Built in 1948, the school once served students in grades 1 to 12. Since then, the district has added a high school and a middle school, largely due to the growing area around Possum Valley. With the addition of each new school, the district has been able to keep up with maintenance needs for the older campuses.

Even the elementary school has seen growth; in the last two years, they have had to add three portable classrooms to the campus to accommodate the population growth.

At one time, the Possum Valley School District had a very simple process for taking care of maintenance requests. Whoever needed work done at a campus, whether administrator or teacher, picked up the phone and called the maintenance department for what was needed. Many times, educators made a request if they ran into one of the men from the maintenance department in the community—at the grocery store, the diner, or even while getting gas for the truck.

Getting the work done was no problem.

Because the district grew so quickly, the district administration had to implement a request and work-order process for the maintenance department. Gone were the days of asking for a can of touch-up paint and getting it by the end of the day, even if the maintenance worker dropped it off at a teacher's or administrator's house later that evening.

Now, whenever a water pipe burst, a fuse blew, or a campus needed touch-up paint for a wall, an employee had to make a request in writing. The work order went into a queue, and each request was taken care of in chrono-logical order, no exceptions.

And for the most part, it worked. The system was particularly effective for any administrator who could plan maintenance requests in advance—or who didn't mind waiting a few weeks to have something repaired.

Mr. Smith followed the work-order protocols. He usually anticipated needs and made requests well before work needed to be done in and around his building, except for one incident.

Last week, he had begun to notice an odor in one of the classrooms. It was a subtle smell, but of what, he wasn't sure. Mr. Smith dismissed the smell, thinking it would go away.

At the beginning of this week, the smell was even stronger than it had been the previous week. It smelled as though someone had left out a lunch container and allowed the contents to spoil. Mr. Smith mentioned it to Mrs. Willacy, the teacher in that classroom.

"I know. I smell it, too," she said. "I've been looking everywhere for what's causing it. I can't find it."

By the end of the week, the room smelled positively rancid. When the students entered their classroom on Friday morning, they scrunched up their faces and held their noses.

"Pee-yoo," gagged several kids.

Mrs. Willacy walked her students over to the administration office and asked them to wait there. She found Mr. Smith in his office, and she requested that he go with her to her classroom.

Although it seemed impossible, in the short time she had been gone, the room seemed even worse.

Mr. Smith's eyes watered as he walked about the room. The smell was the strongest along the north wall.

"I think it's here. It's coming from the wall itself," he told Mrs. Willacy.

"What is it?" she asked.

"I'll let you know in a minute," Mr. Smith said.

3. Issue

Mr. Smith came back with the toolbox that he kept in his truck. Using a flathead screwdriver, he poked a few holes into the drywall a few feet above the ground where the odor seemed the strongest.

Waves of the smell poured out, nearly knocking him over.

After prying away some chunks of the wall, Mr. Smith grabbed a flashlight and peered down into the space between the wall studs.

There were the remains of a possum that had somehow fallen inside the wall space and died.

Mr. Smith went back to his office and logged a work order into the district maintenance request system. The computer screen blinked back at the estimated time it would take to get to this job: six days.

Six days!

That would mean that the weekend would come and go, and the classroom would continue to stink well into next week, not to mention that the deceased mammal was creating a health hazard.

Mr. Smith decided that he had to take action. He was no carpenter, but he had done a few weekend warrior projects in his day. He was sure that he could handle the possum himself.

After school was over, the principal tied a kerchief around his nose and mouth, grabbed his toolbox and a plastic bag, and went to the offending classroom. Using the screwdriver and a hammer, Mr. Smith chiseled away until he had cleared a three-foot-square area of drywall.

Wearing gloves, Mr. Smith disposed of the possum and then looked around at the drywall on the floor. He couldn't use the scraps for two reasons: they were too small, and they reeked.

He would need another sheet of drywall, and he certainly didn't have it at the campus. Before leaving Possum Valley Elementary, Mr. Smith grabbed a couple of blank checks from the campus activity fund checkbook. He would need them when he went to the hardware store.

4. Dilemma

Mr. Smith used one check from the school's activity fund to purchase the supplies he needed to repair the classroom wall. He paid for a sheet of drywall, tape, and other repair materials. He threw in a candy bar and a soda for himself, thinking he would need the energy boost.

On the way back to the school, Mr. Smith also picked up dinner since he would be working late at school that night. Again, he made the purchase with a school check. He planned to write down the check information in the checkbook registry next week.

Mr. Smith returned to his campus, quickly ate his supper, and got to work replacing the drywall. As he was enjoying his candy bar, he realized that he probably should have treated the studs because the smell, although faint, was still there. Upon closer scrutiny, he also noticed that he had left some fairly wide gaps between the new drywall and the old.

His repair job was going to need repair. Mr. Smith thought about calling Mrs. Willacy's husband, Greg, and paying him to repair the botched job on Saturday. Greg had a remodeling business and was always looking for quick jobs.

When Mr. Smith described the work to Greg over the phone, the builder said he'd be happy to help out, for $1,150.

"No problem," said Mr. Smith. "I'll write you a school check. You know it will be good."

They both laughed.

5. Questions

1. What were the first steps Mr. Smith should have taken when the smell was discovered?
2. What policies, if any, did Mr. Smith violate?
3. How should Mr. Smith have planned for and accommodated the instructional needs of all students?
4. Why do you think that hiring Greg Willacy is a poor decision?
5. When can a principal authorize checks from the student activity fund and for what purposes?

1. A Failure of Leadership

Grade Level: Suburban Elementary School, Grades K–5

Standards: 4a, Curriculum, Instruction, and Assessment; 9a, j, Operations and Management

2. Background

Mrs. Jimenez is in line for a promotion. She is principal of Green Acre Elementary School, but she could soon be assistant superintendent for the school district. Mrs. Jimenez has been a dedicated teacher and is only five years away from retirement. She believes that she will get the promotion based on her work over the years. She has confided to a friend that she is worried about the direction of the school. Resources are scarce, and she is particularly worried about the quality of some of the young teachers.

Green Acre Elementary School, like most schools, has a mix of experienced and inexperienced teachers. Many of the older teachers are excellent teachers and have helped the schoolchildren to consistently score high on state assessments over the years. These teachers believe in teaching the three Rs. However, the younger teachers have a poor attitude, and they are often late. It seems that they are not interested in teaching the three R's and leave that to the school enrichment program.

The new teachers use the latest technology, videos, and gadgets to teach. They believe in using projects and group work to teach the students, which is fine, but they have not been giving students homework or increasing rigor in the classroom. The younger teachers are staying within the curriculum guidelines but not teaching enough content and therefore not keeping up with the pacing of the curriculum. As a result, their students have not been passing the mandated state tests at the end of the year.

One younger teacher, Miss Barrett, unlike her younger colleagues seems to be a success. She was hired by Mrs. Jimenez because she was highly recommended by her university. At the year-end standardized tests, Miss Barrett's class scored much higher than average—exceptionally high. This pleased Mrs. Jimenez greatly. However, there were soon complaints about Miss Barrett and her students when her class progressed to second grade.

One day, Mrs. Jimenez was shocked by one of her own teachers. Mrs. Jones, an experienced and much respected teacher, accused Miss Barrett of professional misconduct. She asserted that Miss Barrett had been "coaching" her students. Miss Barrett knew the questions beforehand and encouraged her students to prepare for them. Mrs. Jones believed that the test scores did not accurately reflect the achievement of the teacher or the pupils.

This was confirmed by Mrs. Jimenez when she questioned the new teacher of Miss Barrett's former class. She learned that the children had problems even reading and writing and that they appeared to have learned nothing in the year with Miss Barrett. The high results achieved by the students in Miss Barrett's class increasingly seemed to be the result of her coaching her class, as Mrs. Jones stated, and not of the students' hard work or Miss Barrett's effective teaching. This is a serious example of unprofessional conduct.

It soon became clear to Mrs. Jimenez that there was a series of problems that went undetected by her for some time. Yet she is aware that there is something very wrong with Miss Barrett and her teaching methods. Mrs. Jimenez notices that Miss Barrett had not been using the same teaching materials, but nothing seemed very wrong. It soon appears that Mrs. Jimenez was not aware of the generally unsatisfactory nature of Miss Barrett's classes until notified by the other teachers.

3. Issue

There are three issues in this case study.

The first is that, as principal in charge of management and leadership, Mrs. Jimenez has clearly failed to recognize that there were serious problems with Miss Barrett. It took a colleague to alert her to the fact that not only was the young teacher's class poorly managed but she was acting in an unprofessional way by coaching her students. Mrs. Jimenez is undecided about how she should deal with Miss Barrett.

There is also the issue of how unrepresentative the test scores were of the students' achievements and of the teacher's abilities. The high test scores achieved by Miss Barrett's students contrast sharply with their present behavior and abilities. The tests do not reflect their learning outcomes; this is a serious failing because problems in their education and learning have not been detected because of the high test scores.

The third issue is how to deal with Miss Barrett and ensure that she and the other young teachers follow the rules. It seems that many of the younger teachers tend to do their own thing. They ignore the rules and the accepted practices. This unwillingness to follow acceptable practices may be the root cause of the problem with the exaggerated test scores. If Miss Barrett had followed the rules, she would not have coached her students.

4. Dilemma

The school principal not only confides in her assistant principal but also asks her what she should do. She clearly wants the promotion to assistant superintendent and believes that it would be a fitting reward for her thirty-three years of service. Now she is worried that if she acts against Miss Barrett, she may lose her upcoming promotion. Yet she is acutely aware of her duty to her children—what should she do? Should she put her professional prospects before the school?

Then there is the problem of trying to ensure that all the younger teachers and the older teachers can work together. At present, they are not working as a team, and this means that standards are slipping. The older and younger teachers have very different styles, and this is problematic. This is causing tensions among the teachers, and the children are not receiving a consistently high standard of education.

5. Questions

1. Has Mrs. Jimenez failed to show leadership?
2. How important is it that the test scores reflect the students' abilities?
3. Why is it important that both the younger and older teachers follow the same standards?
4. Should Mrs. Jimenez report the problems with Miss Barrett's test scores to the relevant authorities even though it may have repercussions for her career?
5. How should Mrs. Jimenez respond to the problems raised concerning Miss Barrett?

—*၈/၈/၈*—

1. High Mobility, Low Tolerance

Grade Level: Urban Elementary School, Grades 3–5
Standards: 9 i, j, k, Operations and Management

2. Background

Leslie Atwell became the principal of Eastside Elementary, a Title I school, this academic year. Eastside was known for being a good school, but it wasn't yet an outstanding school like Westside or Northside Elementary Schools. Those two schools always performed well on state assessments, and the curriculum and assessment directors at central office always spoke highly of the campuses.

Miss Atwell wanted Eastside Elementary to become one of those well-respected schools. During her first few months in her new position, Miss Atwell worked diligently at becoming known to the parents in the community. She wanted parents to know that they could trust her with their children's education and that she cared deeply for the students at her campus. She especially wanted to learn more about the environments her students were coming from and what concerned parents most.

As a result, Miss Atwell made quite a few home visits; she always took a teacher or a counselor with her. Her faculty joked that they had never done so many home visits until Miss Atwell became the principal.

Traditionally, the parents at Eastside Elementary had never attended many of the school's events. Many of the families were humble, and they had always felt uncomfortable in the presence of professionals like teachers and especially the school administration.

It was Miss Atwell's goal to change all of that and make the school more accessible to those who lived in the Eastside attendance zone. With the help of the teachers and counselors who went with her on home visits, she was doing that. Gradually, parents began coming to school meetings and felt comfortable talking to the teachers and even the principal.

As the year progressed, the school registrar noticed an uptick in school enrollment. The school had always had a high mobility rate due to some of the conditions the families faced. Many were one paycheck away from being homeless, and when catastrophe struck, families were thrown into the streets and at the mercy of other family members, friends, and charitable organizations.

Yet somehow, in spite of the hard times, they managed to send their kids to school. Eastside welcomed the children, making sure they received meals twice a day and received the best instruction they could deliver.

Now there were more families wanting to register their children at Eastside Elementary. Miss Atwell was sure that it was because of her being inclusive and creating an instructional environment where all children could be successful and feel nurtured. She knew her teachers were doing a fine job with instruction, too. Miss Atwell and her staff created a learning community where kids could be successful, so of course parents wanted their children to attend Eastside.

Last Tuesday, two new families joined the school. Miss Atwell wasn't present to greet the families.

The first family enrolled their son, Billy, a ten-year-old from another district. Miss Atwell made a note to remind herself to contact the family after she talked to Billy's former school. She recognized the name of the school and the principal and looked forward to the call.

The next family, the Maxwells, registered three of their children, one in each grade at Eastside. No one seemed to know much about the family; they had offered scant educational records, having homeschooled their children off and on during their early instructional years.

Miss Atwell decided that she would make a home visit to welcome the Maxwells to the school community.

That afternoon, Miss Atwell called Billy's former principal to find out more about his academic progress.

"Academic progress?" roared the principal at the other end of the phone call. "You ought to be far more worried about his behavior. You oughtta hear what that little tyrant did while he was here."

Within the week, Miss Atwell began to hear stories about Billy's behavior. He had been spreading them himself at school.

It wasn't long before Miss Atwell heard that Billy had taken a gun to his previous school.

Miss Atwell began hearing other stories, too, and these were about the Maxwell kids. Several teachers complained that the kids smelled as though they hadn't bathed in a long time, and the school nurse found that they all carried lice.

These two new enrollments weren't the only ones, however. Several parents were transferring their children from the other elementaries in the district, but they were unhappy about having to do it.

"That other principal, he don't want us there anymore," said one of the parents. "Said we don't live in that zone and can't attend that school."

Miss Atwell explained that students went to the school in their zone of attendance.

"Yeah, well, apparently it was okay for us to be out of the zone until state assessment time. Now they want us all to move where we're supposed to be," said the parent.

"Happens this time of year, every year," said the registrar. "Campuses look at the students they know won't pass state assessment, and then they do home visits to verify where they live. Because the district frequently redraws the zoning for each school, families living along the edges of the school zones have to move."

"Schools like Westside and Northside are targeting kids?" asked Miss Atwell.

The registrar shrugged her shoulders. "Yup, those principals have been doing that for some time. They always get away with it, too."

Miss Atwell thought about that for a moment. How many of the students in her school zone were actually supposed to be attending another school, like Westside or Northside? And if there were students in this predicament, how many were predicted to pass their state assessments, and how many were predicted to fail them? Could the last-minute transfers be why Westside and Northside always had the highest ratings in the district—and even in the city?

3. Issue

Miss Atwell is facing an influx of students at Eastside Elementary. During her first year as the principal at Eastside, her goal has been to create a welcoming community.

Miss Atwell called the former principal of one of the new enrollees, Billy, and became involved in a conversation about Billy's behavior instead of his academics. The Maxwell family has a history of transient behavior, with school not being one of their top priorities. Because of their family's high mobility, no one knows much about them.

It doesn't take long for stories to begin surfacing about Billy and about the Maxwell children.

In addition, disgruntled parents are now enrolling their children in Eastside because they were "called out" by the administration at Westside and Northside for not living in the designated attendance zone.

These aren't the only new enrollees at Eastside Elementary—just a week before state assessments will take place. Miss Atwell now faces as many as thirty new students in her school, all in the course of a single week.

4. Dilemma

Miss Atwell faces three challenges.

First, if it is true that Billy took a gun to his previous school in another district, then he should have been expelled for the remainder of the school year, according to state law.

Second, the Maxwell children have not bathed and are carrying lice in their hair.

Finally, Miss Atwell has learned that the other school principals in her district have identified students unlikely to perform well on state assessments and confirmed that they live in the Eastside Elementary school zone; they have told the families that their children must attend Eastside.

The Eastside teachers will have one week to prepare the new enrollees for state assessments.

5. Questions

1. What should Miss Atwell ask Billy's former principal?
2. What should Miss Atwell do about the stories Billy is telling?
3. Now that the Maxwell children have been identified as having head lice, what are the school's next steps?
4. Should Miss Atwell also identify children in her school zone and require that those who are unlikely to pass their state assessments be sent to the appropriate school?
5. Who could Miss Atwell talk to about the ethics of the Westside and Northside principals? Should she mention this practice or let it go?

—◦/◦/◦—

1. When It Rains, It Pours

Grade Level: Rural Elementary School, Grades K–5
Standards: 9d, e, h, Operations and Management

2. Background

Donna Fishman was a young principal who loved not only her students but also the campus to which she had been assigned. Newell Elementary was named after one of the prominent leaders in the community. Robert Newell was a decorated World War II veteran who had given as much back to his community as he had to his country in the war. When the big flood came in the early 1990s, he had worked alongside many younger men to help rebuild homes in the community. Newell served tirelessly in civic organizations, and he also oversaw several nonprofit boards. He never met a stranger, and the people in the community loved and respected him.

The school district honored Robert Newell by naming a school after him. He was able to attend the dedication of the building before he died. In the years following Newell's death, parents and students alike still talked about the man's legacy to the community. They were proud to attend a school named after someone so wonderful.

Mrs. Fishman was equally proud to be the principal of Newell Elementary; this was the flagship campus of the district. As such, the district did everything possible to make sure the building and grounds were in excellent shape. "Don't worry about a thing," the district maintenance people had told the principal. "We'll handle this for you." This sense of pride seeped into every aspect of campus life, including academics and instruction.

The students consistently scored well on their state assessment exams, and the faculty was relentless in their pursuit of excellence—so much so that they earned the coveted Blue Ribbon designation, a recognition that put them in an elite category of top-performing campuses.

The Blue Ribbon award ceremony was coming up soon. The district invited not only local dignitaries, like the mayor and other political officials, but also several of Robert Newell's family members.

As principal, Mrs. Fishman delegated responsibilities for the program to teachers. The student choir would sing, and selected students would assist with the program itself, from leading the Pledge of Allegiance to introducing the speakers at the ceremony.

The rehearsals had gone well. The students were polished. The day before the awards ceremony, Mrs. Fishman and her head custodian, Ted Horst, walked the campus to ensure that everything was ready for visitors the next day. After visiting every room, including the cafetorium, where the chairs had been set up for the assembly, they were satisfied that the next day would be perfect.

Late that night, however, a tremendous storm blew into the area. Vicious winds and pelting rain ripped limbs from trees, and most people stayed home that night, waiting for the storm to pass. Around midnight, Mrs. Fishman received a phone call from the alarm company.

"We've been trying to get a hold of several other people on our list, but we can't seem to get through. Their phones may not be getting reception. You were the next one on our list to call—sorry to wake you," said a voice on the other end of the phone.

"That's okay," said Mrs. Fishman. "What's wrong?"

"Well, we're getting a message that the west door of the campus is ajar."

Mrs. Fishman smiled. Of course it was the west door. "Yes, that door can be tricky. Sometimes the wind hits it just right and blows it out of the latch, but the chain keeps the door from blowing completely open. I'll go check it out."

The school was less than ten minutes away, so Mrs. Fishman grabbed her flashlight. Her German shepherd sat expectantly by the door. He was almost a year old, neither a puppy nor an adult dog, but an excellent companion nonetheless.

"Yes, come on, Beau," she said. "You can come, too."

When Mrs. Fishman pulled up to the school, she didn't see any suspicious activity. She took Beau inside the school so she could look around. She walked over to the cafeteria. Soon a second light flashed, and Beau let forth a deep, throaty growl as a figure stepped into the room.

"Mr. Horst, it's you!" said Mrs. Fishman. Was she ever glad to see the head custodian.

"Yes, the alarm company left me a message on my phone. I just got it and came right over. Was it the west door again?" he asked.

"Yes, I think so. I hadn't gotten that far yet." Mrs. Fishman took another dozen steps forward, when she noticed she was splashing through water.

"What's this?" she asked. She and Mr. Horst both shined their flashlights at the floor, following the water's path.

"Ah, look," said Mr. Horst. "It's coming from the kitchen area. See how it seems to be flowing from under the double wooden doors here? Watch carefully. You can see the water moving."

"I hope it was just a faucet that was left on," said Mrs. Fishman.

"Yeah, me, too," Mr. Horst responded. "Somehow, though, I don't think that's the problem. We're going to have to shut off the water; the valve is behind that door."

"Open the door so we can get to it."

"I don't have a key to this area."

Mrs. Fishman stared at him blankly. "You don't have a key to the kitchen? Why not?"

Mr. Horst shrugged his shoulders. "I don't know. They said the kitchen belongs to the cafeteria people. Custodians don't clean the kitchen—the cafeteria ladies take care of all of that. I thought you would have a key. You're the principal."

"I don't have a key," said Mrs. Fishman.

"Great. Now what?" said Mr. Horst. "I've been trying to call maintenance—no one is answering their phones."

"Do you have a screwdriver and a hammer?" the principal asked. "Take the pins out of the hinges in the door. We'll take the doors off the hinges and turn off the water."

3. Issue

Even though Newell Elementary is well cared for, there's a tricky west door that sometimes blows open. In this case, the door blew open during a big storm that passed through the area. Both the principal and the head custodian responded to the alarm company's call that there had been a breach in campus security. It was likely nothing important but needed to be checked out.

When the principal and the head custodian, Ted Horst, arrive at the campus, they go to the cafeteria. They find standing water and water still flowing from the kitchen under the doors.

Neither of them has a key to get into the kitchen and close the water valve, but they have to shut off the water to prevent further flooding and ruining the next day's award ceremony.

4. Dilemma

Neither the principal nor the head custodian has been given a key to the kitchen, and yet water is coming from under the doors. Allowing the water to sit may warp the floor, and it will certainly ruin the Blue Ribbon ceremony that is to take place in another twelve hours.

They cannot reach anyone from maintenance to come with a key.

Mrs. Fishman, the principal, directed Mr. Horst to remove the doors from their hinges so they can get into the kitchen and shut off the water. They have broken into an area of the school that was clearly off limits.

5. Questions

1. Should Mrs. Fishman have directed Mr. Horst to break into the kitchen area to shut off the water? Why or why not?

2. Should Mr. Horst have followed his principal's directive to remove the doors from their hinges?

3. Should the district have given the principal or the head custodian a key to the kitchen area? Why or why not?

4. What if the school employees were unionized? How would Mrs. Fishman and Mr. Horst have responded differently?

5. What, if anything, could the principal and the head custodian have done to prevent this situation?

6. What kind of liability would Mrs. Fishman have faced if Beau attacked Mr. Horst and bit him? What about the school district?

1. Stroller Parents

Grade Level: Suburban Elementary School, Grades PK–5
Standards: 8b, f, Meaningful Engagement of Families and Community; 9e, Operations and Management

2. Background

Belinda Smith is the principal at Brookside Elementary, and this is her first position in administrative leadership. After working with the teachers on the school's mission and core values, she and her faculty decided that meaningful family engagement and community were important components of their program; they wanted to nurture the school's relationship with the community.

The previous principal felt that parents got in the way of the educational process and that their presence during the school day made it nearly impossible for the teachers to deliver quality instruction. As a result, he banned parents from visiting the school unless they were invited to the building for a meeting.

Mrs. Smith and her teachers were going to change that.

Frustrated parents wanted to be a part of their children's education, and because the community was so close-knit, they felt that they had been told they were unwanted. This sentiment was particularly evident among parents of the younger children, especially those in pre-kindergarten and kindergarten.

This year, Brookside Elementary invited parents to an open house and orientation before the school year began. Parents could come and meet the teachers; learn about the books and materials the students would be using; and visit the library, cafeteria, and gym.

They could also meet the other parents, which was a great way to get to know the families of their children's classmates.

Separation anxiety between young mothers and their children can be very strong, so during the open house, the pre-kindergarten and kindergarten teachers invited the parents to visit the classrooms during the first two weeks of school. The parents were ecstatic that they would be allowed at the campus during the instructional day.

On the first day of school, there was a flurry of activity as parents escorted their young children to the classroom. The teachers and their assistants were ready with a variety of engaging activities, and the moms stood around the edge of the classroom, watching the teaching and helping to correct their children when necessary.

On the second day, the parents joined the teachers in the classroom again. The classroom had twenty students, a teacher, an assistant, and another ten to twelve anxious parents encouraging their children and offering to "help" them learn. The mothers and fathers took pictures of their children and their classmates, posting them on social media sites.

By midday, the teachers let Mrs. Smith know that there were entirely too many people in each classroom. They simply couldn't teach. Principal Smith went to each class in the afternoon, motioned to the parents to join her in the hallway, and she explained that, starting tomorrow, they would have to remain in the hallway instead of inside the classroom. Having so many people in the classroom at one time was a distraction and a safety threat should an emergency evacuation be necessary.

When the third day of school began, the pre-kindergarten and kindergarten parents came with strollers filled with purses and backpacks, lunches, and a few books to read.

When Principal Smith walked into the early-childhood hallway, she was stunned by what she saw. On both sides of the hall, there were strollers lined up all along the walls except at the classroom doorways. The parents were gathered at the doors of the rooms where their children were inside; each one took turns waving at his or her child through the door window.

Again, they were taking pictures of the first few days of school.

In the afternoon, the principal came down the hall and informed the parents that they could not bring strollers to school. They were impeding traffic, and the fire marshal would not allow it.

Several of the parents were upset and wanted to know why Mrs. Smith was going back on her word. It wasn't fair. And they posted their feelings about the situation on social media, saying that the principal didn't wanted parents to see what really went on in the classrooms.

Mrs. Smith assured them that that was not the case. The parents were welcome for the duration of the first two weeks of school, just as she had promised. She could be trusted, and she would not go back on her word.

The next day, Mrs. Smith didn't even get to the early-childhood hallway to see the teachers, the students, and their parents. Several of the parents were already in the office, demanding to see her.

The teachers, it seemed, had covered up the door windows so the parents and children could not see each other. This was a travesty, they pointed out, and clearly something must being going on that the school didn't want the parents to see.

The social-media posts about the situation increased, and Mrs. Smith wasn't sure if she should respond to them or not. She had never been in a situation like this, and neither had the teachers.

She knew she was going to have to make a statement on social media, however, when she saw the parents attacking other students in the class. They said things like "See how my child is doing so much better than his friend? It's all about good parenting!" When one of the students soiled his jeans and had to go to the nurse, a parent took a picture of him and his damp pants, adding the caption "too embarrassed for this kid—shame!"

Mrs. Smith had to do something and do it fast.

3. Issue

Although the principal invited parents to come and observe during the first two weeks of school, she did not realize how quickly it would get out of hand. More parents than expected showed up, and when they impeded instruction in the classroom they were sent into the hallway. Once in the hallway, they blocked the halls with strollers. They were told to leave the strollers at home and became irate the next day because the teachers had covered the windows with opaque paper.

Did the principal really want them there or not?

The stroller parents also took and posted pictures on social media of not only their own children but also their classmates.

4. Dilemma

The parents have taken to posting on social media how unfair the principal has been with them, especially since she has gone back on her word several times. They described the campus leader as unfair and a liar. They also posted pictures of other people's children.

Mrs. Smith received a phone call from an attorney saying that his clients were prepared to sue the principal, the school, and the district because their child's identify was revealed on social media.

5. Questions

1. What parameters should the teachers and the principal have put in place before school started? Why? Was two weeks too long for the parents to come and see instruction? Why or why not?
2. Does Mrs. Smith have the right to exclude strollers from the school? Can she exclude social media?
3. Do parents have the right to post pictures of their children on social media sites? What about other people's children?
4. What should Mrs. Smith tell the parents who are posting these pictures online? If she joins the social-media conversation, what should she say to the parents?
5. What should Mrs. Smith say to the attorney?
6. What do you think is a better way to encourage parental involvement?

1. Celebratory Gunfire

Grade Level: Rural Elementary School, Grades PK–5
Standards: 9c, d, k, Operations and Management

2. Background

Mandy Longview enjoyed being the principal of Starville Elementary. The school was a rural campus, tucked away at the edge of the district.

Starville was an older campus that had been in use for decades. The stairs creaked when the kids ran up and down, and sometimes the windows rattled during storms. Speaking of storms, any time the area was expecting a heavy downpour, someone had to go to the computer lab on the second floor and place buckets and trashcans in strategic locations because the roof leaked.

The leaks were by no means small. When it rained, they poured. The water coming into the computer lab was so predictable that the principal, the custodian, and several of the teachers knew exactly where to place the receptacles.

Ms. Longview turned in work orders each year for roof repairs or replacement. Each year, maintenance came to the school and repaired the roof, but a roof replacement was out of the question. It was too expensive, said the district. Every year, it seemed as though there were more holes in the roof, in spite of the repairs.

And yet, Ms. Longview loved the quirkiness of the campus. She also liked the community.

Starville Elementary sat alone in what seemed like the middle of a field. In reality, most of the land next to the school belonged to one of the ranchers. The several acres of adjacent land were fenced but largely unused. A small community of homes sprawled out on one side of the campus. The homes were on large lots, compared to what homeowners might find in the suburbs.

Beyond this singular neighborhood were larger tracts of land; there were a few other neighborhoods as well that extended far past the first one.

The community had deep roots in Latin America, and the residents continued many of the traditions from their countries of origin. The school encouraged these celebrations of heritage, observing special holidays and cultural traditions. The principal and teachers invited parents to come to school for these holidays, and the children loved the chance to show off their heritage.

One of the most cherished traditions took place off campus when school wasn't in session, but the celebrations affected the school greatly.

The community residents liked to celebrate New Year's Eve with a big bang, quite literally.

On the last day of the year, many of the men staggered outside in the final hours of the night with their firearms, loaded them, and fired into the sky. In years past, the men usually fired one or two rounds from their shotguns or maybe an occasional pistol. Now that AR-15s were available, it was easy to fire off thirty rounds into the air quickly. The bullets returned to Earth quickly, too, traveling at speeds of several hundred miles per hour.

The bullets rained down in the one area with no one in it on New Year's Eve: the school. No wonder the roof had new holes every year.

When Principal Longview learned why her school's roof had holes in it, she knew she had to change the way the community celebrated the new year.

In January, Ms. Longview set aside an evening for an important parent meeting. The meeting title was "School Safety," and a good turnout was expected.

Sure enough, hundreds of parents came to the meeting, anxious to know about school safety.

"We have a problem," began Ms. Longview. "And the problem lies with some of the practices in the community. I'd like to talk to you about those tonight, and I have a short presentation to show you."

The parents became very silent as Ms. Longview showed pictures of the school's roof, riddled with holes. Next, she showed pictures of the computer lab. She was proud of being able to upgrade the computers, and she showed pictures of the students on the computers in the lab. They were engaged in learning, and they looked as though they were enjoying what they were working on.

Next, the principal showed a picture of the computer lab during a storm. There were no children in the pictures, just computers and trashcans catching water coming in from the ceiling.

"When it rains, the children cannot be in the lab. It's too dangerous for them because of the leaking roof," said Ms. Longview. "I also worry about the damage to the technology your tax dollars have purchased."

She continued, "I want you to stop discharging weapons on holidays. This practice is harming the school building. If you are not careful, you may also harm a child or each other."

There was a murmur in the audience. Finally one parent stood up.

"Does that go for everyone?" asked the parent.

"Yes, of course. I want you all to be safe," said Ms. Longview.

"Then you better tell your fifth-grade teacher Mr. Salinas that he better stop shooting into the air, too."

All heads turned and looked at Mr. Salinas.

"Hey, I want to have a little fun on New Year's Eve. What's the harm?" Mr. Salinas asked. "Besides, Marco shoots, too."

"Marco?" asked Ms. Longview. "Our assistant principal?"

3. Issue

Starville Elementary has holes in the roof, and every year new holes appear. Most of the holes are right over the computer lab. When it rains, the ceiling leaks, preventing students from using the lab and endangering the equipment.

Discharging weapons into the air as celebratory gunfire is a cultural tradition in the community. It's also a serious crime to fire a weapon into the air. The sheriff can't be everywhere on New Year's Eve to arrest offenders. Not only are they damaging the school, but the bullets are a serious threat to life.

4. Dilemma

When Principal Mandy Longview met with the parents for a safety meeting, she clearly outlined the challenges that celebratory gunfire could cause. Ms. Longview painted a compelling picture of the damage some of the members of the community caused with their ballistic partying.

Then one of the parents asked if she wanted her fifth-grade teacher and assistant principal to stop firing guns in the air, too.

Now Ms. Longview has to confront two of her employees, both present at the meeting, about their behavior in the community.

5. Questions

1. How can Ms. Longview convince the district that her school needs a new roof?
2. What are the dangers of celebratory gunfire? Should the practice be encouraged, even if it's part of the community's heritage?
3. What was good about Ms. Longview's presentation at the school safety meeting? What else could she have done?
4. When is the best time to meet the teacher and the assistant principal about discharging weapons toward the school on holidays? Is Ms. Longview overstepping her bounds? Why or why not?
5. What other school-leader standards are relevant to this case? Why?

Chapter Five

Family and Community Engagement

—⟨∿∿⟩—

1. I Gotta Be Me

Grade Level: Rural Elementary School, Grades PK–5
Standard: 7e, Professional Community for Teachers and Staff

2. Background

Principal Donna Bates looked at the number that was flashing on her phone. It was human resources calling her, and that was odd this late in the day. Usually that department had shut down and gone home.

Principal Bates picked up the phone.

The HR director was on the other end, and she needed a favor, a really big one.

"You still have that fourth-grade opening, Mrs. Bates, and I think I have a teacher for you," said the director. "He's from another campus, he didn't get off on the right foot, and I think he needs another chance, a second chance. You're the only person I could think of to do that. Please say you'll take him."

Mrs. Bates sighed. She had done this favor for central office before. Several of the people she had helped with second chances became very successful in their careers in the district and beyond.

"Okay," said Mrs. Bates. "But I want time to meet with him first—before he goes into a classroom of mine."

"Whatever you need," said the director.

Larkin Mulweather reported for work the next morning. He was tall and lanky, with a genuine big smile. He seemed likeable enough. He liked working with kids. He was comfortable teaching the fourth-grade curriculum. He never really had any problems with classroom behavior management.

"There's gotta be something," thought the principal. "We just haven't found it yet."

She took Mr. Mulweather to his classroom and showed him where his supplies and materials were. Then she gave him the key to the classroom.

Principal Bates checked in on Mr. Mulweather a couple of times throughout the day. All seemed to be going well. The students were engaged in the lesson, and Mr. Mulweather seemed to be a good teacher.

The rest of the week went by without incident. Friday afternoon, the HR director called.

"How are things?" she asked.

"Mr. Mulweather?" asked the principal. "He seems fine. Class is going well. The kids seem to like him. It looks like we're good."

The next week, Mr. Mulweather stopped by Mrs. Bates's office. "You look good with your hair up, he said. "Have you thought about trying a French twist? I can show you how . . ."

"No, I'm good," said Mrs. Bates. Was that it? He likes styling hair?

By midweek, one of the second-grade teachers came to complain about Mr. Mulweather. He had been telling her that he knew just enough magic— good magic—to help cure the bunions on her feet. With a simple spell and ten minutes of her time, the teacher would literally be back on her feet in no time. All he needed was an egg from the cafeteria. And a broom.

Mrs. Bates called Mr. Mulweather to the office.

"Okay, got it," he said. "No hair styling, no magic spells."

Again the rest of the week went by without incident. So did the next one. Then the HR director came by for a campus visit.

"Let's go see for ourselves," said Mrs. Bates. Together the two made their way to Mr. Mulweather's classroom. From the outside, it sounded as though the teacher was leading the students in some sort of review game.

The two administrators went into the room. A tall woman was at the front of the room. Her long ash-blonde hair was tied back loosely with a ribbon. She wore a knit shirt, a knee-length skirt, and wedges.

"Oh no," whispered Mrs. Bates to the HR director. "I didn't realize that Mr. Mulweather was absent and had gotten a sub."

One of the students leaned over to whisper to the principal. "That's not a substitute. That's Mr. Mulweather. He likes to dress like that."

The principal and the HR director took a closer look. The figure appeared to be extremely similar to Mr. Mulweather's. Same height, same gestures. She even had the same ability to teach a class and engage the students consistently.

"Can I help you two?" asked Mr. Mulweather.

"Yes, Mr. Mulweather, please come by my office when you get a chance," said Mrs. Bates.

"Oh, I'm not Mr. Mulweather today. I'm his alter-ego, Ms. Mulweather," said the teacher.

When Mr. Mulweather came to the office, Mrs. Bates was ready to have a conversation with him. After talking to the HR director, she knew that in addition to having poor boundaries and wanting to fix his colleagues' hair or cure their conditions, Mr. Mulweather was a cross-dresser.

He sat down in front of the principal's desk and crossed his legs. "Is this where you tell me I can't be a cross-dresser, either?" he asked the principal.

3. Issue

The HR department has identified a teacher as a poor fit at one campus in the district, and now they want to reassign him to another campus.

Principal Donna Bates agrees to allow him to take the open fourth-grade position she has, but she discovers that this new teacher has some quirky behavior.

4. Dilemma

Mr. Mulweather has crossed a boundary by offering to fix his colleagues' hair and cure their ailments. Each time the principal spoke to him about his behavior, he corrected it. This time, however, the principal finds Mr. Mulweather teaching his class while cross-dressing.

5. Questions

1. What questions should Mrs. Bates have asked about the new teacher?
2. What should the HR director have said about Mr. Mulweather?
3. Was Mrs. Bates right in correcting Mr. Mulweather's actions resulting from his poor boundaries?
4. What should Mrs. Bates tell Mr. Mulweather about cross-dressing in the classroom?
5. What, if anything, should Mrs. Bates tell the parents?

1. Same Old, Same Old

Grade Level: Rural Elementary School, Grades PK–5
Standards: 7f, g, Professional Community for Teachers and Staff

2. Background

Every year, the Pleasant Valley School District meets in August for their annual convocation, professional development training put on for the teachers by district personnel. Every year, the high school hosts the program, and lunch is brought in for all of the teachers who attend the training.

All employees gather in the gym, where the superintendent addresses the faculty and staff gathered from every campus across the district. For an hour, he talks about how he spent his summer and what plans district has for the upcoming year. Next, he invites each principal to the microphone so he or she can say a few words.

The messages from the principals are always positive and upbeat, and they never vary from year to year. This year, as Principal Bill Blighton of Jones Elementary made his closing remarks, he advised his faculty, "Keep your eyes open, and you'll learn something over the next three days."

There was polite applause, and like the other principals, Mr. Blighton returned to the bleachers to join his faculty.

Next, everyone received printed schedules and maps of where all the breakout sessions were being held. Every teacher had to attend the offered session in each of the following areas: curriculum, instruction, assessment, behavior management, technology, and employee benefits. The breakout sessions were offered in the mornings and in the afternoons for the next three days. The teachers had to get the initials of the presenters to get credit for attending the sessions.

They were the same sessions offered last year and the year before. In fact, they were the same sessions that had been offered every year that the superintendent had been at the district. It was the same old, same old.

Mr. Blighton made the rounds, visiting every one of the sessions his teachers attended on the first day. He was there to see the teachers, and he wanted them to see him as well. The faculty was attending the sessions, but many were dividing their attention between the presenter and their mobile phones.

On the second day of professional development, Mr. Blighton made it to each of the morning sessions, but then just before lunch, he joined several principals for a conversation about the new bus transportation routes that the district proposed. Some of the principals were less than happy about the neighborhoods that would be in their new attendance zones.

Lunch was over before they knew it, and they decided to leave the high school to grab a decent lunch. The meal took longer than expected, and when they returned to the high school, the day was nearly over.

On the third day, Mr. Blighton hung around the cafeteria for a while, eating donuts and drinking coffee. Just before lunch, he went to check on his teachers. He again visited every session, but he didn't see many of his faculty in attendance. They had to be somewhere, he thought.

On the fourth day, after the professional development at the high school building was finished, the Jones Elementary teachers were to meet at their own campus. Mr. Brighton had a meeting scheduled first thing in the morning. He collected his teachers' training certifications, noticing that every faculty member had all six sessions initialed. The rest of the day had been set aside for the teachers to review students' cumulative folders and prepare their classrooms.

During the meeting, the teachers were looking at their phones, laughing, and texting, just as they had been doing during the professional development days at the high school.

The principal asked what was going on, but everyone put away their phones for the time being.

When the teachers had been released to go to their rooms, the librarian stopped by Mr. Blighton's office.

"I can show you what's going on with the teachers," she said. She held out her mobile phone, which already had an app open on it.

Mr. Blighton put on his reading glasses so he could read the writing.

"The thread begins back here," said the librarian. "When you said 'Keep your eyes open, and you'll learn something over the next three days,' a teacher posted your comment, and immediately afterward something else wrote 'Keep our eyes open—that's a good one, LOL! I may fall asleep.'"

The principal scrolled down a little.

"Fall asleep? I already z z zZ ZZZ," said the next message.

Mr. Blighton kept reading. His teachers had made fun of the superintendant's remarks and then the man himself. Next, they turned their attention to their own principal.

"Anyone seen BB yet?"

"Our session, urs next" and "Coast is clear" were some of the responses.

"So much for eyes open and learning. Where is everybody?"

"Lunch" and "shopping" were some of the most popular responses. "Seen this b4" and "Been there, done that, don't want the t-shirt" were also in the message thread.

Mr. Blighton pulled his glasses from his face. Clearly, the reason he had not seen his teachers on the third day of district-led professional development was that they weren't even present.

And yet all of their forms had been signed.

The phone in Mr. Blighton's rang, and he picked it up.

"Can you please explain why my secretary is showing me a picture of myself with 'Stay boring, my friends' written across it?"

It was the superintendent.

3. Issue

Every year the teachers from elementary, middle, and high schools in the district attend the same staff development in Pleasant Valley School District. They meet for three days of professional development; each year, exactly the same information has been given out during the sessions.

Also each year the teachers must update their health insurance information and sign another acceptable-use policy to use any of the district's technology.

The teachers have requested in the past to be allowed to have collaborative sessions with one another so they could align and plan instruction better. The district has denied their requests each year.

4. Dilemma

Principal Bill Blighton has discovered that his teachers did not attend all of the required sessions offered by the district, and yet every one of them had the required initials. Mr. Blighton has proof that the teachers were elsewhere.

Many of the teachers have been making negative comments about the district training, the superintendent, and even the principal on social media.

Now the superintendent also wants to know what was going on; he has just seen a meme that makes fun of him.

5. Questions

1. Mr. Blighton attended some but not all of the professional development sessions himself. How likely is it that his behavior influenced his faculty's behavior? Should he have attended the sessions with them? Why or why not?
2. What should Mr. Blighton do about the forged professional development sheets?
3. How should Mr. Blighton handle the comments made by his teachers on social media?
4. What recommendations do you have for the district's annual training?
5. If the district ignores suggestions from the principals, what can the principals do?
6. What should Mr. Blighton tell his superintendent about the meme?

1. Don't Drink the Water

Grade Level: Rural Elementary School, Grades PK–5
Standards: 7b, c, d, Professional Community for Teachers and Staff

2. Background

Nurse Nina Garcia had been working at Lee Elementary longer than Larry Huston had been a principal.

Now in his third assignment as a campus administrator at an elementary school, Mr. Huston liked how well his school ran, thanks to the systems he put in place. He began by hiring the most competent and qualified staff he could find, although Lee Elementary already had many of the positions filled. There wasn't very much staffing for him to do because so many of the faculty and staff returned each year without fail.

He put systems in place that minimized paperwork and saw to it that efficiency ruled. He didn't like busywork, and he didn't want his teachers to have to do it, either.

The other thing Principal Huston didn't like was a lack of trust. He wanted his teachers and staff to able to come to him any time to discuss problems they were having in the classroom or with their jobs. He also liked it if they brought several solutions they were thinking about implementing.

Mr. Huston would listen and ask them questions, and usually the employee came up with the right solution on his or her own. The principal felt that he was building leaders at the campus, and many of the employees appreciated that. In the past, they had always been told what do you, and now they were being encouraged to take a little ownership and practice their leadership skills.

This attitude permeated more than the teaching staff—the cafeteria workers tried to solve their own problems, and so did the custodians. Even the school nurse would come by to visit with Mr. Huston to talk through several solutions.

The principal's policy was, if the door's open, I'm available.

That's why it was a surprise on Thursday morning when Mr. Huston was closing and locking his door just before school was about to start.

"Mr. Huston?" asked a voice. It was Nina Garcia. "I think I have a problem."

"Oh good morning," the principal said. "I'm on my way to this week's leadership meeting at the central office. Door's closed—can it wait?"

"Um, I don't know," said the nurse.

"Well, it's going to have to—I'm late as it is. But I'll be back this afternoon. Let's meet then," said Mr. Huston.

And with that, he was out of the building, leaving Mrs. Garcia behind. She returned to her office.

At the leadership meeting, the principals in the school district were being assigned plenty of tasks for the upcoming week. There were reports to fill out, materials and information to distribute to teachers, and reminders about the upcoming custodians' meeting and the community night out.

As each one came across the table to him, Mr. Huston was texting various staff members back at the campus with messages like "Heads up—textbook inventory due in two weeks" to the assistant principals and "Pick up audiometer Friday" to Nina Garcia.

The other principals were doing the same thing—texting to let their staff know what important things had to be taken care of. It was almost like a competition to see who among the principals could get their staff to finish first.

After lunch, Mr. Huston glanced at his phone. He had heard back from everyone but the school nurse. That was odd.

What was even odder was the message he received from his secretary. It said, "I think you better come back to campus right now. It's about Mrs. Garcia, and it's urgent."

Did the nurse need a nurse? Mr. Huston stepped into the hallway to call the school and then couldn't believe what the secretary told him.

"Mrs. Garcia has labeled every water fountain at the school with a sign that says 'Contaminated. Do not drink the water.'"

"She did *what*?" he blurted out. "How many people have seen those signs?"

"Apparently a lot because there are quite a few parents outside in the parking lot. They are holding up signs about the water. They're picketing."

Mr. Huston quickly looked at the Lee Elementary social media page; the nurse had posted the warning there, too, and the parents were already commenting on the post.

Principal Huston asked to speak to the superintendent outside the meeting.

She assured him it would be okay to leave the leadership meeting and go back to the campus. "And call me to let me know how it turns out," she said.

When Mr. Huston pulled into the campus parking lot, he saw that there were indeed about twenty parents marching in a circle and holding up signs about the contaminated water on campus. As soon as they saw the principal get out of his car, they swarmed around him.

"What are your plans for the water? How thirsty are our children going to be? What if they become dehydrated?" the parents asked.

"First of all," said Mr. Huston, "no one will become dehydrated. We always keep bottled water on hand for emergencies. Remember that our building also serves as a community shelter, so we have plenty of water on hand. Second, we're not sure that the water is contaminated. We'll have to wait and see. This is the first I heard of it."

One of the parents filmed and posted the speech to a social media site, saying that obviously Principal Huston was so out of touch with the campus that he didn't know about the contamination; in fact, he didn't even come to work until midafternoon, and his attitude was one of wait and see. In the meantime, he was jeopardizing their children's health.

3. Issue

School nurse Nina Garcia has taken it upon herself to identify the water in the school water fountains as contaminated. She based her information on a notice sent out by the water-supply company, which said there could be elevated risk for some chemicals in the water, but the water was safe to drink at this point.

The nurse put signs on every water fountain alerting everyone that they should not risk their lives and drink the water.

4. Dilemma

Mr. Huston is returning to the campus from a district meeting when he runs into a band of picketing parents in the parking lot. They ask him a barrage of questions, and he answers them, but one of the parents takes the answers out of context and posts the remarks on social media.

The superintendent and the parents are waiting for answers, but Mr. Huston hasn't even gotten inside the building yet.

5. Questions

1. Did the school nurse overstep her role and take the idea of leadership too far? What if the water really was contaminated?
2. What would you have advised Mr. Huston to tell his secretary? Should he have gone inside his building via the back door so that he would miss the picketing parents?
3. What should Mr. Huston tell the school nurse? Should disciplinary action be taken?
4. How would this situation be different if Mr. Huston had listened to the nurse earlier that morning?
5. What follow-up should Mr. Huston take? Why?

1. Where's My Kid?

Grade Level: Rural Elementary School, Grades PK–5
Standards: 8j, Meaningful Engagement of Families and Community; 10a,
School Improvement

2. Background

Maggie Hernandez, the principal at Garcia Elementary, knows that many of
her students are in the United States without permission. She has seen parents
driving cars with foreign plates drop off their children at the school. The
parents cross the border every day so their children can come to school at
Garcia Elementary.

It is well known at Garcia Elementary that quite a few of the students are
using a cousin's or a friend's address to enroll in the school. Even though she
knows it's happening, Ms. Hernandez does not say anything.

The teachers at Garcia Elementary prefer not to make home visits of the
students in their classrooms. In their experience, the effort is wasted because
the parents they really need to speak to are never at the listed location. Some
of the teachers complain that these parents are accessing other services they
are likely not entitled to because they are not citizens.

Principal Hernandez's stance has always been that, wherever the students
came from, they are in Garcia Elementary now, and it is the school's duty to
care for the children during the day and to educate them. Immigration and
welfare validation is not the school's concern, Ms. Hernandez reminds her
teachers. Their concern is education, nothing more, nothing less.

Denise Tucker is a fourth-grade teacher at Garcia Elementary. She is one
of the teachers upset by the undocumented status of some of the children. She
has made it well known that she is opposed to undocumented children coming across the border for a free education. "They take benefits meant for
citizens," Ms. Tucker insists. "And it's not fair."

Ms. Tucker blogs at her website, which is called Americans for America.
She routinely writes about immigration issues, citing facts and statistics
about the immigrants' imposition on America. Recently, the blog posts have
been coming very close to the issues going on at Garcia Elementary.

Although she hasn't mentioned Garcia Elementary specifically in a post,
she has alluded to the situation at school.

Principal Hernandez pulled into the school parking lot one morning and
noticed that the cars bringing students to school were not entering the drop-

off area but were stopping outside the gates, causing the children get out in the street and walk through the parking lot to the school building.

Ms. Tucker was standing in the drop-off lane, holding her mobile phone up to take a video of the arriving cars' license plates.

Ms. Hernandez went over to Ms. Tucker. "You do not have permission to do this," the principal said. "Stop filming and go inside; you have no right to do this."

Ms. Tucker shrugged her shoulders and did as she was told. During her conference period, however, Ms. Tucker posted the video she had taken that morning to her blog site, along with defamatory language about the influx of students, the laws protecting them, and her administration.

Ms. Hernandez was busy dealing with another situation that had arisen. Child protective services had come by just before lunch and checked a child out of school in order to continue an investigation they were working on.

Someone had reported that a fourth-grader, Lisa L., was likely being abused. When child protective services came to pick Lisa up, they checked her out from the campus, promising that they would provide her with lunch and that they would bring her back to the school before the end of the day so that she could ride the bus home as usual. The parents would not know that there was an investigation until it was time to bring them into it.

An hour before dismissal, Lisa's mom came to Garcia Elementary to pick her up for a medical appointment. When the office worker called Ms. Tucker's classroom to request that Lisa come to the office to go home for the day, Ms. Tucker said, "Lisa's already gone for the day. Don't you remember the social worker came and took her?"

Lisa's mom overheard the conversation between the office and the classroom.

"Excuse me, but did the teacher just say that my daughter has *gone* for the day?"

The office worker didn't know what to say.

"Where is my daughter?" the parent started screaming. "What have you done with her?"

Hearing the commotion, Principal Hernandez stepped into the reception area. "Please join me in my office," she said. "We have something to talk about."

The principal assured the mother that her daughter was fine and showed her in the sign-out system that Lisa had been checked out several hours ago. This is routine, the principal reassured Lisa's mom. It happens all the time, especially if there's an investigation.

"An investigation!" said the parent indignantly. "My child is being investigated? For *what*? Because she's too white? Apparently that's it, because look at who you would rather have enrolled in your school: illegal immigrants!"

With that, Lisa's mom held up her phone. The video from the morning was playing in a continuous loop. It was the video that Principal Hernandez told Ms. Tucker to stop making.

Sure enough, Ms. Tucker stopped filming exactly when she was told to, but she posted the video on her private blog. Lisa's mom had seen the video and the blog. So had 187 other people who liked or loved it.

3. Issue

At an elementary school with a large population of illegal immigrants, the teachers have been told that they are not to expose who these students are. It is the school's obligation to educate them with all their other students, even though the families do not pay taxes. One parent has the opportunity to confront Ms. Hernandez about the situation.

4. Dilemma

Lisa's mom had come to the school to pick up her daughter an hour early. Lisa had a medical appointment. The mother was at first angry and offended that her white daughter was being held as if a witness in an investigation. Also, she insisted, no one should be allowed to take a child off campus without the parent's permission, especially when no one would do anything about the illegal alien situation at the school. Why is it that those children come before the children of law-abiding parents who pay taxes for the school?

To top it off, the parent had proof in the video that Ms. Hernandez forbade the teacher from making but that was later posted online.

5. Questions

1. Can and should Ms. Hernandez reprimand Ms. Tucker for posting the video? Why?
2. Do the children of illegal immigrants have the right to a free and public education?
3. Does a protective-services agency have the right to remove children from campus for all or part of the day without parental consent?
4. What should Ms. Hernandez tell the parent? What should she tell Ms. Tucker?
5. How should the principal handle the video that has been posted?

1. When Push Comes to Shove

Grade Level: Suburban Elementary School, Grades PK–5
Standards: 8a, b, Meaningful Engagement of Families and Community

2. Background

Several years ago, Littleton Elementary revamped their behavior-management program. The teachers and school principal, Betsy Russ, met to decide the best approach and together selected a more positive method of managing behavior and disciplining the students at school.

The discipline data they collected prior to the change told them that there were a considerable number of discipline referrals; in one year alone, the six hundred–student campus had accrued nearly two thousand discipline referrals.

Some of these referrals were for minor infractions, such as not bringing pencils and other supplies to the classroom or not completing homework assignments. Other referrals were for more serious infractions, like fighting, vandalism, and bullying. The lesser infractions did not result in any disciplinary action.

Fighting and vandalism usually resulted in out-of-school suspensions. Many of the referrals for bullying indicated that the bullies had been referred to the counselor, but no further action was taken.

The new behavior-management program was designed to reward good behavior when it happened. That meant that the faculty had to decide what that behavior would be and how they would reward it when they saw it.

Each grade level identified the behaviors they wanted to see and then presented them to the rest of the faculty. As a group, the faculty decided on school-wide behaviors and how to teach them. The teachers even planned the kind of incentives they wanted to use.

The next step was to decide on the consequences for any infractions. Principal Russ insisted that students should not be written up for failing to bring a pencil to class. Instead, most of the lesser infractions could be handled in the classroom by the teachers. Most of the teachers agreed with the principal's assessment. Only a few teachers still wanted to send kids to the office for any discipline problem.

One of the teachers who felt this way was Eva Dinsley, an experienced teacher who still remembered when corporal punishment was used in the classroom.

"And it worked, too," she reminded the other teachers whenever she got the chance. She also tried to remind them that it was the administration's job to handle discipline problems. Her job was to teach.

"I don't let anything come between me and instruction," said Mrs. Dinsley. "No kid is gonna keep me from a lesson."

Principal Russ and the discipline committee met monthly to review the data collected.

They began to notice an interesting trend. Office referrals were way down; as the year went by, there were fewer and fewer referrals to review. Even Mrs. Dinsley was writing fewer referrals than before. Suspensions were down, too, as were incidents of bullying. It appeared that the new behavior-management system was working.

Principal Russ was caught completely off guard by what happened next.

The parents of Mary Lamb came to meet with the principal to talk about what had been going on in the classroom—Mrs. Dinsley's classroom, to be specific.

Mary was the victim of bullying, and apparently the bullying had been going on for a long time. Several of the boys in class had been teasing her because of her height. Not only was she the tallest girl in class, she was the tallest student. The boys called her names like "Giant," "Amazon Girl," and "Giraffella."

The Lambs explained that Mary reported the bullying to her teacher, Mrs. Dinsley. Sometimes Mrs. Dinsley told the boys, "Stop it," or "What you really need is a good spanking." On a couple of occasions, the teacher said, "What do you want me to do about it? It's not like I can write a referral anymore. You're stuck with it, and so am I."

"I had no idea," said Principal Russ. "Of course I will look into this immediately."

The principal had several more meetings to attend after her meeting with Mr. and Mrs. Lamb, and by then it was the end of the day. She would meet with Mrs. Dinsley tomorrow.

The next day, Mrs. Russ forgot to meet with the teacher. In fact, it wasn't until the end of the week that she remembered about Mary and her parents' complaint.

Mrs. Russ called Mary to the office. Although the girl was tall, she acted as though she wanted to disappear into the fabric of the chair itself. She slouched and let her hair hang over her face. For every question Mrs. Russ asked Mary, the girl answered in a soft voice that could barely be heard.

Next, the principal met with Mrs. Dinsley to find out what was going on.

The teacher sat with her arms folded across her chest. "Yeah, some of the boys act up. They're boys, and that's what they do."

"What redirection have you given them?" asked Mrs. Russ.

"I told them they better stop," said the teacher.

Satisfied with the answers, Mrs. Russ let it go at that.

The following week, the school nurse asked the principal to come to her station. She had one of Mrs. Dinsley's students, Peter Marks, with her, and he was probably going to need stitches on his forehead.

"What happened?" asked Mrs. Russ when she saw Peter holding a compress to the side of his head.

"I got pushed into the water fountain," he cried.

"Who did this?" asked the principal.

"A girl," said Peter. "It was Mary!"

3. Issue

Mrs. Dinsley did little to stop the bullying in her classroom. She told the class bullies to "stop it" when they called a fellow classmate names but did nothing else.

Concerned about the bullying, the girl's parents told the principal about it; the principal said she would take care of it. By the next week, however, the bullying had continued, and the girl took the problem into her own hands. She shoved one of the boys into a water fountain, where he got a gash in his head that required stitches.

4. Dilemma

The school district has a zero-tolerance policy for bullying and for physical aggression.

A student who has been a victim of bullying has taken matters into her own hands; she has shoved one of her bullies, causing serious injury. The bullying had been going on for some time in Mrs. Dinsley's classroom.

The principal must call the parents of both students, and she'll have to follow through with consequences for their actions as well.

5. Questions

1. What should the principal's first response be? Which parent should she call first? What should she tell each of the parents?
2. What consequences should the children receive?
3. How should Mrs. Russ follow up with Mrs. Dinsley?
4. What other data could the discipline committee have reviewed to determine trends in behavior?
5. Where did Mrs. Russ fall short in following up with the accusation of bullying?

Chapter Six

Case Study Resolutions

CHAPTER 1: ON A SCHOOLING MISSION

Resolution to Duty Schedules Case Study

Grade Level: Suburban Elementary School, Grades PK–5
Standard: 1c, Mission, Vision, and Core Values

Asking the teachers to coordinate their instructional schedules, lunches, conferences, and duty times and stations was far more to take on than the faculty could handle. When it came down to the planning, they were not ready for a leadership challenge like this.

Ms. Ennis took responsibility immediately for the failed initiative rather than blame the teachers. The teachers did not have enough training or experience in writing school-wide instructional schedules. Giving them a master schedule with more specific parameters might have been helpful. For example, they could have planned how each block of time for mathematics or language arts would be used. By not preestablishing the master schedule for art and music, chaos would result.

Placing the children's needs first and foremost would have helped the scheduling. For example, older students can generally eat lunch later in the day than younger students.

Ms. Ennis could resolve the conflict in a variety of ways, including team-building activities, a change of task and place, and allowing teachers to work in their grade levels. Teacher leaders could assist in the areas of instructional design, finding resources, mentoring, and so on.

Resolution to Survey Insights Case Study

Grade Level: Urban Elementary Charter School, Grades PK–5

Standards: 1b, f, Mission, Vision, and Core Values

Principal Michaelson was on the right track in wanting to get input from his teachers, parents, and surrounding community as they prepared to create a vision for the Best Charter Elementary School. Although he felt as though he knew what his team would say, getting their formal input was an important step in getting buy-in for the work ahead.

The superintendent's revised surveys skewed the possible results. The campus survey was more than doubled in size and focused on central-office administrators and their work. The parent survey was significantly reduced in size. In addition, the superintendent intended to use the survey results for administrator evaluations. This was not the purpose of the survey.

Mr. Michaelson was correct in asking his nonexempt employees to take the survey as part of their paid work hours. Asking an hourly employee to work outside the regularly scheduled day is still considered work time, and they must be paid for the time. To do otherwise is a violation of labor laws.

Mr. Michaelson should share the survey results with his campus. Possible discussion topics include how perceptions have been illuminated and what suggestions the campus would like to make in moving forward. It's likely that the campus will make suggestions that only central office can approve because of the top-down approach the charter district has taken.

This top-down approach seems to be misaligned with Mr. Michaelson's philosophy of educational leadership. He might choose to have an honest conversation with the superintendent about the direction in which the district is headed, or he might decide to polish his résumé and search for a district more aligned with his educational philosophy.

Resolution to Workroom Whispers Case Study

Grade Level: Suburban Elementary School, Grades PK–5
Standard: 1c, Mission, Vision, and Core Values

Any employee who feels as though they have been violated or harassed has the right to speak out. The outcry should go to the immediate supervisor, but if the employee does not feel comfortable doing that, he or she may cry out to anyone.

Mrs. White must talk to the teachers and make it clear that their behavior must stop immediately and that continuing to belittle and harass colleagues will not be tolerated under any circumstances.

The principal should not address the teachers as a group in the workroom. Instead, she should talk with each one in her office. This defines the issue as a serious one, and it also maintains privacy. It is more professional to discipline the teachers in private than in front of their peers. The rationale for stopping the behavior can be tied to the school's mission, vision, and core values.

It would be wise to send Mrs. Gonzalez and the other teachers to diversity training as well as sexual-harassment-prevention training.

Resolution to Viral Video Case Study

Grade Level: Urban Elementary School, Grades PK–5
Standards: 1g, Mission, Vision, and Core Values; 2d, Ethics and Professional Norms

Mr. Blackwell should immediately contact every parent of Mr. Johnson's students to let them know that he is not in the classroom today and that the class will have coverage by a certified teacher. Mr. Johnson's views do not represent those of the district nor of the school. Mr. Blackwell can inform the parents that he will explain more by the end of the week, but for now, the students are in a safe learning environment.

Next, Mr. Blackwell should call central office for support from public relations (handling media requests) and from security (to handle crowds of people if necessary). The principal should tell his office staff to forward all media requests to the public relations officer. He must also inform his teachers that they are not to post information about the incident on their own social media sites.

The next step is to work with human resources in drafting a letter placing Mr. Johnson on leave pending the results of an investigation. The letter may be sent as certified mail or through personal courier, but a signature showing the receipt of the letter must be obtained.

Inciting a riot and demanding the killing of people is a felony offense, for which Mr. Johnson can be removed from his teaching position. He can also lose his professional teaching certificates, a request that either the human resources director or the superintendent must make. Mr. Blackwell may not get a chance to reprimand Mr. Johnson for misrepresenting the reasons for his absences; it would have been better to have a conversation about them as soon as Mr. Blackwell thought there might be a problem.

First Amendment rights do not extend to anarchy and civil unrest. Although Mr. Johnson has the right to protest, he does not have the right to incite disorder, mayhem, and murder.

Resolution to Fifth-Grade Follies Case Study

Grade Level: Urban Elementary School, Grades K–5
Standards: 2b, d, e, Ethics and Professional Norms

When Ms. Garcia returns to school, she should immediately meet with the assistant principal to find out what happened at the talent show performance. Next, she should interview several other people.

Finally, she will need to meet with Miss Redman. Ms. Garcia must make it clear that Miss Redman was insubordinate by not following her principal's directive to change the song and dance routine to something more appropriate. Ms. Garcia should also point out the inappropriateness of the gown Miss Redman wore to the show. This determination should also be documented in writing. It's always advisable to have another person present in the meeting to take notes. In this case, it should be the assistant principal.

A final step would be to contact whoever posted the video and ask that it be removed because it violates the privacy of minor children.

Ultimately, Ms. Garcia may want to consider sending a letter home to parents regarding the school's position on the talent show and resulting social media posts, inviting parents to contact her directly with concerns.

Resolution to Sticks and Stones Case Study

Grade Level: Urban Elementary School, Grades PK–5
Standard: 2e, Ethics and Professional Norms

Mr. Franklin likely explained to the Stanfords that their child's records were legal documents and as such must have the legal name on them. That includes school records, such as a permanent file and report cards. The school personnel could, however, refer to the student by the preferred name, much the way some students go by a nickname.

Is was a good idea to have the counselor lead the orientation because she may be working closely with Mike during his education at this school. Mike could get to know her and she him, and the parents may feel that they have another school support.

Mr. Franklin was right to call the teacher, but as a follow-up he should also have sent an e-mail stating only the facts of the situation. He should have also been on the alert when the teacher called in sick that Monday, perhaps asking the counselor or an assistant administrator to start the class so that everything got off on the right foot.

The principal should call the parents to let them know what happened and how the school will be handling the situation.

Resolution to Because I Said So Case Study

Grade Level: Urban Elementary School, Grades PK–5
Standards: 2a, b, Ethics and Professional Norms

Mr. Franklin would have done well to collaborate with his teachers at the beginning of the year to set the campus goals. Getting teacher input also gets buy-in. The teachers would be far more vested in achieving a goal they set as a team because together they could hold each other accountable for reaching it. They would be more likely to help each other, too.

It is possible that several of the teachers made up or inflated their grades so that Mr. Franklin would stop badgering them about students who were failing. While most teachers are honest, responsible, and transparent about issues such as grading, there may be a few who invent grades, especially if their boss is adamant about passing grades being the only way to measure learning success.

Mr. Franklin should have explained what he meant by stating that all children would pass. As the campus leader, he would have noticed when tutoring was taking place and which teacher was offering it. Comparing a tutoring schedule with the teacher roster may tell him who is tutoring and who is not.

At that point, Mr. Franklin could hold private conversations with the teachers with whom he may have concerns. It would be beneficial to also look at student work samples as they discuss each failing student. Mr. Franklin should not assume that the teachers know what he means, so he should be specific.

While school choice is an option for many parents, sending half of the school to another location may be a strategic impossibility. Mr. Franklin, with the help of the superintendent, may be able to talk the parents into staying, especially if a good community plan is put into place to make sure this doesn't happen again.

Resolution to Not in My School Case Study

Grade Level: Rural Elementary School, Grades K–5
Standards: 1c, Mission, Vision, and Core Values; 2f, Ethics and Professional Norms; 8h, Meaningful Engagement of Families and Community

Because a school employee must look out for the safety of children, Ms. Baumeister had every right and the responsibility to stop the parent who had an open container of alcohol in his vehicle when he came to pick up his children. He was on school property, and alcohol is not permitted on school property. Asking the parent to switch drivers—assuming that his passenger had not also been drinking—was an effective way to handle the situation.

Had the parent refused to comply with her request, Ms. Baumeister could have detained the driver by refusing to release the children to him. At that point, her next step would be to call the local police or sheriff. Had the parent taken his children anyway, she should notify the sheriff's department, who could then pull the parent over and determine blood alcohol content.

Although calling the parent's employer is an option, it is not the principal's place to do so.

Ms. Baumeister must follow up with the accusation about her librarian. She should meet with the librarian and ask her directly about the accusation.

If the librarian denies the accusation, the response should be documented, and Ms. Baumeister should monitor the librarian's behavior.

If the librarian admits to drinking and driving or drinking while at work, Ms. Baumeister should notify the human resources department and follow district policy regarding the librarian's behavior. It's likely that Ms. Baumeister would want to get Mrs. Strand the help she needs to overcome her drinking problem.

CHAPTER 2: INSTRUCTIONAL LEADERSHIP AND SCHOOL IMPROVEMENT

Resolution to Flu Epidemic Case Study

Grade Level: Urban Elementary School, Grades PK–5
Standards: 10i, h, School Improvement

Mr. Gould could have sent out a letter to the faculty and parents advising parents about the rise of the flu and reminding them what steps they could take to prevent getting it, including washing hands.

It was not appropriate for him to spray the school building with disinfectant while the faculty and students were present. It is likely that there were no MSDS (material safety data sheet) documents available for the chemical he was using. He placed the health of others in jeopardy.

A principal should not meet alone with an angry parent if at all possible because the conversation can quickly turn into a contest of hearsay. It would have been better to include an assistant administrator or the school nurse in the conversation instead.

The principal should not lie about attendance. Attendance reporting is a legal procedure. Instead, Mr. Gould should tell Mr. Little that he will not be blackmailed and that he himself will report the incident to the superintendent's office.

Mr. Gould might also want to pick up a box of tissues and some orange juice on the way home.

Resolution to Data Matters Case Study

Grade Level: Rural Elementary School, Grades 3–5
Standards: 4f, g, Curriculum, Instruction, and Assessment

Mr. Zabek should become more involved in monitoring the curriculum, instruction, and assessment process at his campus or collaborate with experts at his central office or at a local education service center.

Developing a predetermined calendar of CBAs and establishing consistent procedures for their administration and review will help teachers plan for instruction and provide students with what they need for improving their performance.

Mr. Zabek could meet with either teacher first but should plan to have a second person take notes for him. This could be his secretary or another administrator. Either way, he will have to confront Mrs. Albertson about her teaching practices, set expectations for improvement, and monitor her progress.

His next steps should be to hold a grade-level meeting with the fifth-grade teachers to review procedures and scores and to establish new procedures for CBA administration and reteaching. He will also have to consistently monitor their progress.

Mr. Zabek should consider regrouping the students so not all special-needs students are in a single classroom. The current placement may be a violation of student IEPs because their placement in Mrs. Davis's class can be interpreted as "self-contained." In addition, Mr. Zabek may want to rethink his choice of lead teacher.

Furthermore, Mr. Zabek should send the teachers to continual professional development that will help them improve their ability to analyze data and revise instruction. Discipline management is another area to consider for professional development. This attention to purposeful, ongoing training may help Mr. Zabek retain high-quality teachers.

Resolution to Story Time Case Study

Grade Level: Suburban Elementary School, Grades PK–5
Standards: 4b, d, Curriculum, Instruction, and Assessment

The purchase could be considered unnecessary, depending on the size of the classroom libraries. A principal should also consider whether the other teachers would want to supplement their libraries. Mrs. Wise could have asked for an itemized list of the books Miss Flynn wanted to purchase as supplementary reading material. If Mrs. Wise did not feel comfortable vetting the list of books requested, she could have asked the curriculum department to do so.

Speaking to the parents individually will allow the principal to hear their concerns in private, provide validation, and seek individualized solutions. Listening to all the parents at once may increase the level of anger because they may feed off each other's fury about the situation.

The books must be removed from the classroom.

It is never okay for a teacher to discuss sexual preferences or practices with students. A discussion like this is highly inappropriate for second-graders. Mrs. Wise should reprimand Miss Flynn, placing written documentation in the teacher's personnel file about the incident. It would be prudent to involve the district's human resources department in the matter.

Resolution to More Than a Day on a Calendar Case Study

Grade Level: Suburban Elementary School, Grades PK–5
Standards: 4b, d, Curriculum, Instruction, and Assessment

Teaching about other cultures and their holidays can be a good lesson in multiculturalism. Unfortunately, the population at Crestview Elementary was not diverse enough to lend authenticity to the holidays, so the teachers had to research and learn about many of the holidays to be able to teach them to the students.

Excluding the traditional holidays celebrated by the community indicated that their traditions and celebrations have little value in the modern world. Some campuses exclude references to Christmas, for example, when referring to "Christmas Break" as "Winter Break." Religious holidays can be recognized as long as there is no indoctrination into the religion or religious observance at the school. Because the school celebrates the birth of the Prophet Muhammad, Mrs. Leon has little argument to keep other religious dates off the calendar.

In addition, categorizing the holidays as offensive because they celebrate white men is as inappropriate as excluding other cultures in lessons about how cultures spread and change.

If the school and the district acceptable-use policies do not permit teachers to engage in social-media activities, then the teachers should not defy the rules.

The superintendent will likely tell Mrs. Leon to work with her teachers and parents to collaboratively come up with multicultural events to celebrate at Crestview Elementary, making these observances more than a day on a calendar.

Resolution to Someone Like Me Case Study

Grade Level: Urban Elementary School, Grades PK–5
Standards: 4a, Curriculum, Instruction, and Assessment; 5d, Community of Care and Support for Students

Mrs. Bradford can send Mr. Upton home for the day. During his absence, she can confer with the human resources department about further action, which will depend on how many infractions he has already accrued. At the very least, it would be wise to document the incident, connecting the infraction to the leadership standards and employee handbook. The issues that need addressing are manhandling a child, ordering a suspension without due process, and calling the students unacceptable names.

Mrs. Bradford should meet with the Blacks and their son. If they have not seen the video, she can reference it or show it to them. Maxwell started the incident but did not deserve to be dragged out of the classroom. A lesser consequence could be school suspension. The parents may wish to press charges against Mr. Upton.

Carlos violated the acceptable-use policy for technology on the campus and should receive appropriate consequences for his actions.

Mrs. Bradford can help Mrs. Owens get the training she needs for better classroom management. Another option is to supplement the literature book with relevant culturally diverse authors.

Follow the social media policy of the district. Dump the coffee.

Resolution to They Read Just Fine Case Study

Grade Level: Urban Elementary School, Grades PK–5
Standards: 10c, e, School Improvement

Mr. Roberts could have introduced the reading specialist at the campus, but the specifics of her role could have been left out. Pointing out her target populations could easily alienate immigrant and nonimmigrant parents.

Mr. Roberts would have done well to intervene early in Mr. Meyers's speech by asking him to cease and desist. The parent should not have been allowed to put down any group. A way to calm down an outraged person is to acknowledge and validate the person's concern. Mr. Roberts could have told Mr. Meyers that he was willing to schedule an appointment with him, or he could have asked the parent to leave the meeting.

Mr. Meyers will likely be charged with assault, should Mr. Roberts wish to press charges, which he has every right to do. Mr. Roberts may request that Mr. Meyers not be allowed back on the campus due to safety concerns— for himself and especially for the children.

There may be nothing Mr. Roberts can do about uploads to social media, but he should refrain from commenting on them because they may be used as evidence.

Resolution to Change Begins Now Case Study

Grade Level: Suburban Elementary School, Grades PK–5
Standards: 10i, j, School Improvement

Because school had not yet started, there was little reason to demand possession of the principal's office. Although the reason for Mrs. Gonzalez leaving is not identified, it would be gracious to allow her to retain her dignity and leave as principal of the campus.

Mr. King could immediately take on the duties of the principalship, including reviewing student and staff rosters, scores, inventories, and the upcoming budget. In addition, he could plan for teacher in-service days and contact organizations in the community for their support.

Mr. King should discreetly report the wine incident to the human resources director or the superintendent. It is possible that they may already
know of the situation. In addition, states and school districts have policies
about receiving gifts from potential vendors.

Mr. King should tell his teachers only what they need to know about his
private life; going into details is not necessary. His sexual orientation cannot
be an issue for his employment, but it would be better to replace the photo of
himself and his boyfriend with one of himself with his dogs because this is an
elementary school.

CHAPTER 3: MULTICULTURAL ISSUES AND CULTURAL COMPETENCE

Resolution to Ticket to Fun Case Study

Grade Level: Urban Elementary School, Grades PK–5
Standards: 3a, d, e, Equity and Cultural Responsiveness

Administrative leave may be the best choice for Mr. Rogers because it
allows the district to remove the employee without judging guilt or inno-
cence. Mrs. Bidwell should have received at least a reprimand for targeting
students from a specific background and neighborhood. Whether she would
also be placed on leave could depend on her previous actions at the school
and whether they had been properly documented.

Mrs. Luhan was wise to show data in support of the new behavior systems. Data can help to separate the program from subjective emotional support. It was also appropriate to remind teachers to select the program most
aligned to theories of child development. Deploying the new program in
installments may have been a good approach. The teachers could implement
each step and gauge effectiveness. Mrs. Luhan should supervise the teachers
and support them in making the change. Had she done so, she may have
discovered much earlier that Mrs. Bidwell refused to implement the new
behavior system.

The principal must confront Mrs. Bidwell's negativity. The teacher's
statements are unprofessional and inappropriate. If she continues to make
such remarks, the principal should document her insubordination. If Mrs.
Bidwell changes her attitude, that should also be noted and placed in her file.

Address the parent concerns by thanking them for bringing up the oversight. The principal could also ask what the parents would like to see happen.
It is likely they want an equitable solution, which may involve getting input
from the other teachers in the grade level. Students in Mrs. Bidwell's class
could be given a set number of tickets based on the grade average distribu-
tion, or they may be allowed to earn double tickets until the school carnival.

Resolution to Rainy Day Recess Case Study

Grade Level: Rural Elementary School, Grades PK–5
Standards: 3b, Equity and Cultural Responsiveness; 8b, Meaningful Engagement of Families and Community

Principal Wallace should direct the PE teacher to create lesson plans centered around health or other activities related to physical education, including reading about athletes or sports figures, identifying healthy habits, and so on.

He could allow Miss Woodward to continue the activities as long as all students are treated equally and given the opportunity to express themselves in the various activities.

Instead of leaving the classroom in the hands of an irate parent, it would have been better to call the office for assistance or to send a student to get the principal. Mr. Wallace should have addressed emergency procedures for situations like this, and there should be procedures outlined in the faculty handbook.

It may be worthwhile to ask the district if it would be possible to enclose the pavilion so that it could be used for PE during inclement weather as well as on nicer days.

Resolution to Bullying on the Bus Case Study

Grade Level: Urban Elementary School, Grades 1–5
Standards: 3a, d, g, Equity and Cultural Responsiveness; 5e, Community of Care and Support for Students

Ms. Jackson must investigate the matter carefully and thoroughly. She could ask the teachers and the bus driver to make written statements of what they saw happen. In addition, there may be camera footage from the bus. This video may also provide clues to what happened.

Being the son of a PTA president or a school superintendent does not excuse bad behavior, especially bullying.

Regardless of how an altercation began, the boys should not have called Keylsie names or removed and defiled her hijab. Posting pictures of Keylsie on social media platforms is a violation, and the Piranis can sue the parents of the boys. They stand a good chance of winning their suit if there is concrete evidence of these pictures.

If it is true that Keylsie provoked the boys by spitting on them first, she will also face consequences according to the district's student code of conduct (standards 3a, d, g).

Although Keylsie is the first Muslim student attending Booker T. Washington Elementary, she will likely not be the last. Ms. Jackson should arrange for professional development on cultural diversity and ensure that all students are welcome at the school. The teacher can then provide lessons on positive student conduct as it relates to the classroom, campus, bus, and beyond. In addition, the faculty can assist in recognizing important cultural holidays of groups other than those already recognized (standard 5e).

Resolution to Sanctuary School Case Study

Grade Level: Urban Elementary School, Grades PK–5
Standards: 3a, c, g, Equity and Cultural Responsiveness

Principal Cruz should explain to the faculty that they have received a directive from the superintendent. She has *not* asked the administrators to keep law enforcement out of the schools. Instead, she has stipulated that there must be a warrant, and the school principal must confer with the school system's legal advisor before taking any action.

The superintendent was right to allay concerns for child safety and assure the community that their children will be taken care of at school. It's important to be aware of inflammatory language like *arrest and deport* and *split apart*. Adding the comment *viva la raza* may be seen as inflammatory and taking sides against populations in the community.

A school is a sanctuary for immigrants, thanks to *Plyler v. Doe* of 1982. This landmark case determined that no child, regardless of origin, would be denied an education. School personnel cannot release information about their students, including their addresses and other personally identifiable data, due to the Family Educational Rights and Privacy Act (FERPA). In some cases, the information is also protected under the Health Insurance Portability and Accountability Act (HIPAA).

If parents refuse to leave the parent center at the end of the day, consult with the school district's legal department.

Although answers may vary in regard to the phone calls from ICE and from the media, no principal or other employee should reveal or release over the phone personal information regarding any child. In both instances, an administrator can refer the caller to (1) the superintendent's office and (2) the public information office.

Resolution to Not in My Classroom Case Study

Grade Level: Rural Elementary School, Grades PK–5
Standards: 3f, g, Equity and Cultural Responsiveness

Mrs. Judson had every right to ask for the removal of the posters from the classroom because they could be seen as proselytizing or showing one religion to be better than another. Secondary-level teachers may include references to the Bible in instruction when teaching allegory or another literary device, but elementary students are not ready for this level of instruction.

It's good that Mrs. Judson is willing to speak favorably of the district's curriculum, but a better approach would have been to assure the parents that every effort had been made to be fair and impartial when teaching about religion and that they are not instructing students *in* any particular religion.

Mrs. Judson should contact the curriculum director to discuss why students must learn an Islamic prayer when no other prayer has been required. It may have been an oversight. Teaching what and how to pray violates the separation of church and state. However, it is permissible to explain how each religion prays. Doing so teaches respect in a diverse cultural context.

If the parents turn to social media, Mrs. Judson cannot stop them, but she could choose to engage and explain, or she could invite the parents for a grade-level meeting to improve understanding.

Mrs. Longmire's alternative activity was appropriate because it still related to the topic. Her final statement is insubordinate, but she will still likely win her case because she had already been directed to remove Bible verses from her classroom; now she is being asked to display verses from the Quran.

Resolution to Left Behind Case Study

Grade Level: Rural Elementary School, Grades PK–5
Standards: 5a, b, c, Community of Care and Support for Students

Riding the bus routes the first week of school was a good idea because it helped the teachers become familiar with the community, and the community took notice that the teachers helped to supervise their children. A principal may strongly encourage riding the buses after school, but teacher's unions or professional organizations may disagree. Nonexempt employees, such as instructional assistants, must be paid for their time. The best practice is to ask for volunteers among the exempt faculty and staff.

Ms. Cantu was right in staying in contact with the transportation department and the parents. She should have checked the rooms much sooner, and it would have been appropriate to call Tyler's teacher to see if she remembered putting him on the bus. In addition, the principal should always call the superintendent to advise him or her of the situation.

Calling the transportation director back to yell at him may make Ms. Cantu feel better, but she should only advise the director that she will be following up with the superintendent regarding the situation. It is unlikely that she will be allowed to speak with the bus driver. The transportation department will discipline the driver.

Ms. Cantu could stop by the home later in the evening to visit the Comptons, but a phone call may suffice. Either way, she should offer school counseling services for Tyler. Under no circumstances should she offer to drive Tyler home. Taking a child home in a personal vehicle could be a liability for the principal and for the district. It is better that a bus take Tyler home if his parents cannot pick him up.

In most cases, there is a district public relations officer who will speak to the media on behalf of the school. The PR officer may post follow-up information on social media sites.

Resolution to Restroom Pass Case Study

Grade Level: Urban Elementary School, Grades 3–5
Standards: 5a, b, Community of Care and Support for Students; 7b Professional Community for Teachers and Staff; 8i, Meaningful Engagement of Families and Community

The principal is right to find ways to accommodate the social, emotional, and physical needs of every student. This means protecting students from bullying and allowing them to use the restroom of choice. A school must, however, keep all students safe, and measures must be put in place to prevent one student from abusing another one. The principal should ask for an investigation into the girls' claims; it would have been better to interview each girl and her parents individually than as a group. The principal must also talk to Alan and his parents (standard 5a).

The school administration should continue to discreetly identify those students with gender-fluid identities. Parents may make this identification known; it is possible that a teacher or a counselor may observe gender-fluid traits in children. Providing the teaching staff with training on the issue may help them identify these students and come up with ways to support them in the classroom (standard 5b).

The administration can also collaborate with the faculty in designing systems that support and document student whereabouts, providing a follow-up for students who may be gone from the classroom too long (standard 7b).

Finally, the school principal and the staff should continue to advocate for the rights of all students. The adults can continue to support the needs of all children, including those who may have acted out inappropriately. While an investigation into Alan's behavior is necessary, it is also necessary to keep information about his behavior confidential.

As for pressing charges, state law applies here. In some states, charges cannot be filed against a student until the age of ten; generally, only a victim or the parents of a minor victim may file charges. The principal will have to follow district policy regarding consequences for behavior. Alan's parents must be notified, and Alan should be referred for counseling.

Resolution to The Red Sweater Case Study

Grade Level: Urban Elementary School, Grades PK–5

Standards: 5a, b, Community of Care and Support for Students

Ms. Conway has some discretion in determining Sarah's punishment for plugging up one of the school toilets with her sweater. Given the circumstances, it's likely that a warning will suffice.

What's more important is to stop the bullying by Billy and the teacher.

The principal, using the pretext of reading a story, allowed Mrs. Grouse to take a break and compose herself. It also gave her time to think about the consequences she might face for yelling at her students.

Ms. Conway should investigate how much yelling Mrs. Grouse is doing. She can interview some of the students individually, including Sarah and Billy. Redirecting Mrs. Grouse in front of her students will embarrass her and cause her to lose even more credibility with her students.

Next, Ms. Conway must meet with Mrs. Grouse and direct her to stop yelling at students and bullying them. This meeting must be documented in writing. Also, Mrs. Grouse should attend cultural-diversity training.

Billy should be reprimanded for bullying Sarah; this reprimand must also be clearly documented.

Most important, Sarah needs plenty of support to get past this incident. A phone call or home visit can explain what happened to the red sweater. Her parents may not know that she refuses to wear the sweater. Refer Sarah to a school counselor regarding her being the victim of bullying. The counselor can also teach an anti-bullying lesson in the classroom and then follow up by evaluating its effectiveness. Finally, the school can give the parents the contact information for agencies that can help out if they are having difficult times.

Document in writing all actions taken.

Resolution to The Field Trip Case Study

Grade Level: Urban Elementary School, Grade K–5
Standards: 5a, Community of Care and Support for Students; 8b, c, Meaningful Engagement of Families and Community

Because the teachers have designed this field trip as instructional time rather than simply a reward for good behavior, all students must be able to attend the trip to the zoo. The teachers must find a way to accommodate every child's behavioral needs as much as they accommodate academic needs. Mr. Holleman's support and guidance is crucial (standard 5a).

However, behavior that would prevent a student from being at school on the day of the field trip could prevent him or her from going on the field trip.

To provide support for the field trip, Mr. Holleman could ask for parent volunteers to also go on the field trip and help with chaperoning the children. A list of volunteers could be created at the upcoming parent meeting. The administration and the teachers must be careful that they do not violate

FERPA or HIPAA privacy standards when talking to parents; they cannot discuss another child's condition (standard 8b).

Other actions could include sending a counselor or junior administrator if one is available, and Mr. Holleman could hold an expectations meeting with each student individually before the field trip.

CHAPTER 4: HUMAN RESOURCE MANAGEMENT

Resolution to Social Media Mavens Case Study

Grade Level: Urban Elementary Charter School, Grades K–5
Standards: 6a, b, Professional Capacity of School Personnel

Ms. McClure would have been wise to check several social media sites to see how the Adams sisters spent their spare time. This check would have revealed they had indeed been working as strippers for several years.

So that teachers do not burn out so quickly, the school could create tutoring camps—designated periods of time, such as two, four, or six weeks—when a teacher commits to tutoring but then takes a break to let someone else step in and tutor for a while.

Ms. McClure could fire the Adams sisters for unsuitable behavior—and for sleeping in class. Doing so would leave two positions to be filled immediately. Ms. McClure could hire a substitute, but that would be a temporary solution. She should build relationships within the community, especially if there is a nearby college, so she can post for her open teaching positions.

To retain teachers, the charter district could offer bonuses throughout the year.

Resolution to Custodial Calamity Case Study

Grade Level: Rural Elementary School, Grades PK–5
Standards: 6b, c, h, i, Professional Capacity of School Personnel

Mr. Johnson should immediately tell Mr. Radgale that the posters are inappropriate for the workplace and must be taken down and removed from the premises immediately. Materials such as these are considered sexual harassment, and they do not belong in a place of work, especially a school.

Furthermore, Mr. Johnson would do well to recommend that Mr. Ragdale attend sexual harassment–prevention training so that he does not make a similar mistake in the future. Mr. Johnson must tell Ragdale that he intends to document the offense in writing but that he will follow up with written documentation that the matter has been taken care of.

Mr. Johnson should notify both human resources and management and facilities that Ms. Connor did not return to work after her approved leave expired. He should continue to contact her for two more days, and if he has not heard from her, he can request that her position be opened. Ms. Connor's lack of response is considered job abandonment.

There should already be a letter on file for Ms. Connor, reprimanding her for insubordination.

Opening the head-custodian position will allow applicants to apply for the job. Mr. Johnson and a committee of his choice can interview candidates and make a recommendation to the board for the hiring of a new head custodian.

As long as Mr. Ragdale complies with Mr. Johnson's directive, he would be eligible to apply and be given an interview for the job.

Resolution to Time for Professional Development Case Study

Grade Level: Urban Elementary School, Grades PK–5
Standards: 6g, h, i, Professional Capacity of School Personnel

Mrs. Wyatt devotes considerable time to her teachers, making sure their needs are met. Coaching can be an especially effective strategy for helping others find solutions as well as setting and achieving new goals. Continued professional development helps teachers stay current in their field.

Mrs. Wyatt should not call her teachers late at night or early in the morning unless there is an emergency, such as a school closure or other catastrophe. Even a digital message like texting may make the recipient think an immediate response is necessary.

As the campus instructional leader, Mrs. Wyatt should continue her own professional development. While administration often requires long hours, working excessively at a campus where systems are in place and operating smoothly leads to workaholic behavior and burnout. It is important to model an appropriate work-life balance for employees to see.

Getting away for professional development can be rejuvenating and rewarding, even if a person has worked in education for a considerable amount of time. Professional development at any point in a career improves effectiveness.

Resolution to Legendary Lothario Case Study

Grade Level: Suburban Elementary School, Grades K–5
Standards: 7c, e, Professional Community for Teachers and Staff

The other school leaders standard this case involves is standard 2. Mrs. Black should not give Logan Keith permission to take Miss Jackson off campus during the lunch period. Because he supervises the instructional assistants, any actions that Mr. Keith takes could be considered sexual harassment. Giving certain employees long-stemmed red roses and being seen in close conversation with an instructional assistant lend suspicion to Mr. Keith's behavior.

The superintendent should have told Mrs. Black that the district might be concerned about Mr. Keith's inappropriate behavior; however, allowing Mrs. Black to discover the behavior on her own meant she had no preconceived ideas.

The campus secretary, Mrs. Smith, may have received a rose because there was an extra one or because Mr. Keith wanted it to seem as though he had given all the women a rose.

Resolution to Playing Possum Case Study

Grade Level: Rural Elementary School, Grades PK–5
Standards: 9c, d, Operations and Management

Mr. Smith's duty is to seek, acquire, and manage the physical resources necessary for instruction. As soon as he and Mrs. Willacy knew that the odor's source could not be identified, he should have logged the maintenance request and also called the maintenance department to explain that this was a health emergency. Failure to act quickly could place the health of children and the faculty in jeopardy.

If the maintenance department did not feel as though the issue merited immediate attention, Mr. Smith's next step would be to call the superintendent and request that this work be an immediate priority. If there is not already a system in place for prioritizing work orders, Mr. Smith can suggest one.

By performing the repair work himself, Mr. Smith did not follow the protocol set forth by the district. It is possible that he also violated labor standards if there is a union in place for the maintenance workers.

Most importantly, Mr. Smith must find space for Mrs. Willacy and her class; a possible solution would be to hold class in the library or the cafeteria until the classroom smell has been cleared (standard 9c).

Mr. Smith failed to act ethically in his stewardship of the school's activity fund. Monies in the student activity fund are generated by students and, as a result, are for student use. Although state laws governing the use of activity funds may vary, in general, student activity funds cannot be used for personal use. Purchasing building supplies, even though for the classroom, may be considered personal use. The candy bar, soda, and certainly dinner at the diner are personal use.

Mr. Smith also neglected to enter the check information in the registry, opting instead to do it later. This also violated policy.

Finally, as a campus principal, Mr. Smith was not in a position to contract work on his own with an outside vendor. By delaying action on the odor in Mrs. Willacy's classroom and then hiring her husband to correct his work, Mr. Smith's collaboration resembles collusion. Again, a student activity–fund check cannot be used to pay for these repairs (Standard 9d).

Resolution to A Failure of Leadership Case Study

Grade Level: Suburban Elementary School, Grades K–5
Standards: 4a, Curriculum, Instruction, and Assessment; 9a, j, Operations and Management

Mrs. Jimenez is duty bound to bring the issue with Miss Barrett to the assistant superintendent and those in charge of assessments at the state level, sooner rather than later, even if it does cost her a promotion. She is ultimately responsible for the situation. There should be a full investigation into the issues.

Mrs. Jimenez should collaborate with her staff to make sure that Miss Barrett's former students are provided with extra help to make sure that they meet the required standards.

The school principal, if she does not receive her promotion, must change the way that she manages the school. She needs to initiate a program that allows all the teachers to work as a team and that ensures they are all adhering to the required standards and practices.

There is a clear division between the younger and the older teachers. The teaching faculty and staff need to be monitored to ensure that they are complying with the standards. The school principal may introduce a mentoring system so that older teachers can help younger teachers.

The new initiatives (standard 9a) will ensure that the coaching of students will not be repeated and that tests will reflect the teachers' and students' achievements. These are very important issues for the school (standard 9j).

Resolution to High Mobility, Low Tolerance Case Study

Grade Level: Urban Elementary School, Grades 3–5
Standards 9i, j, k, Operations and Management

Miss Atwell should call Billy's principal back and find out if Billy had taken a gun to the campus. Any student in possession of a firearm must be reported to the appropriate state agency and local law enforcement before the student is expelled. It would be appropriate to insist on further educational information, including whether Billy had been identified as a special-needs student. Often misbehavior is the effect of poor learning ability. Miss Atwell can also speak to Billy's parents.

If the story proves to be true, Billy will have to be withdrawn from Eastside. If the story is not true, Miss Atwell should meet with Billy and his parents to explain that bragging about taking a weapon to school is unacceptable behavior.

Miss Atwell could direct the school nurse to send the Maxwell children home to have their hygiene needs addressed. Another option would be to wash the children's hair with lice-removal shampoo at school. Either the school nurse or a teacher could call child protective services to report a case of possible neglect if the parents are unresponsive to the situation.

Targeting students likely to perform poorly on standardized high-stakes assessments is an ethics issue, and Miss Atwell should gather the facts based on enrollment this year and prior years and report the situation to her immediate supervisor and the superintendent of schools.

Resolution to When It Rains, It Pours Case Study

Grade Level: Rural Elementary School, Grades K–5
Standards: 9d, e, h, Operations and Management

Breaking into the kitchen area allowed the head custodian to turn off the water that was flooding the cafeteria. The flooding was an issue not only because of the upcoming prestigious awards ceremony but also because of the damage the water could do to the floors, causing an even greater expense.

The custodian should not have this, even though the principal directed him to. And in such a situation, both employees should have been present and on camera (if one exists in the area), proving that they simply turned off the water and did not tamper with anything else—or take any of the food in the kitchen.

Because of high rates of food theft and stringent federal and state requirements, many districts do not allow anyone but cafeteria leaders to have keys to this area. If this is the requirement in a district, a principal may have little influence on who gets a key to this area. The principal can, however, act in the best interest of protecting district property and open the doors. The action must be reported to the appropriate personnel.

Calling local law enforcement to respond to the situation—or at least to meet the principal and the head custodian at the campus—would have been appropriate.

If the campus employees were unionized, no employee could overstep his or her job duties. The cafeteria would have been flooded when everyone arrived at the school, and an emergency cleanup crew would have had to come out to prepare the room for the ceremony—or move the ceremony to another location.

Had Beau bitten Mr. Horst or anyone else, Mrs. Fishman would have assumed all liability for the dog's actions. The district has no liability for an employee's dog.

Resolution to Stroller Parents Case Study

Grade Level: Suburban Elementary School, Grades PK–5
Standards: 8b, f, Meaningful Engagement of Families and Community; 9e, Operations and Management

Mrs. Smith and the teachers could have invited parents for a predetermined block of time—perhaps an hour in the morning and an hour in the afternoon. They should have clearly outlined in writing what would and would not be permitted in classrooms or in the hallways, including strollers. Two weeks was too long for the parent visitation, especially because there was such a large group.

Mrs. Smith may exclude strollers from the campus for safety reasons. Excluding social media is much harder. She can only ask parents to refrain from posting, but she can also tell them why it's not a good idea to post pictures of other people's children if they do not have permission.

Posting the pictures of another person's child may jeopardize the safety of that student, especially if the child is considered a ward of the state or is named in a custody battle. It would have been wise to explain these considerations to the parents at the open house. Mrs. Smith had every right to defend herself in social media forums as long as she did so professionally.

The school could encourage parent involvement by opening up a parent resource center where parents could help teachers and assistants in preparing projects and learn about school initiatives and parenting strategies.

Mrs. Smith should collect the attorney's information and state that she will get back to him after speaking with the superintendent of schools.

Resolution to Celebratory Gunfire Case Study

Grade Level: Rural Elementary School, Grades PK–5
Standards: 9c, d, k, Operations and Management

Ms. Longview could arrange to show her presentation to the superintendent and the director of maintenance and facilities. Pictures of the leaks in the roof and ceiling could be compelling. She might even have the opportunity to show the presentation to the school board. In that case, she could ask parents to go to the meeting to support the request.

Celebratory gunfire is dangerous, and those engaging in it should stop because of the potential for injury or death. It is illegal to engage in celebratory gunfire in most communities.

Ms. Longview did well to include pictures that told the story of the roof and resulting leaks. She might have also requested a representative from the sheriff's office to add to the serious tone of the meeting.

It's inappropriate to meet with school employees about their behavior in front of the parents. The principal should, however, meet individually and in private with them the next day regarding their actions. Although they are not on campus when firing their weapons, the teacher and the assistant principal cannot shoot at the school.

The standard of professional ethics dictates that educators must uphold standards of professional conduct, including avoiding engaging in criminal activity. The principal is not overstepping her bounds in talking to her employees about their off-campus behavior, but she cannot reprimand them for their actions.

Committing a criminal offense, such as illegally discharging a weapon, falls under professional ethics PSEL standard 2.

CHAPTER FIVE: FAMILY AND COMMUNITY ENGAGEMENT

Resolution to I Gotta Be Me Case Study

Grade Level: Rural Elementary School, Grades PK–5
Standard: 7e, Professional Community for Teachers and Staff

Mrs. Bates should have asked why Mr. Mulweather was being moved. Be sure to drill down for specifics by asking open-ended questions that provide more than a yes or a no answer.

The HR director should have mentioned some of the more prominent behaviors, such as cross-dressing. If the teacher is on a growth plan, the principal needs to know that.

Explain to Mr. Mulweather about boundaries and clearly outline the expectations for his behavior. Follow up frequently to check that he is consistently meeting the expectations that have been set.

Permitting teachers of fourth-graders to cross-dress is not a good idea. The concept is not appropriate for this age group. If Mr. Mulweather insists on cross-dressing, he should plan to do so on his own time rather than on school time.

Mrs. Bates might want to send a letter home with the students explaining that their teacher likes to dress up at times in class.

Resolution to Same Old, Same Old Case Study

Grade Level: Rural Elementary School, Grades PK–5
Standards: 7f, g, Professional Community for Teachers and Staff

It is generally recommended that principals be present for their faculty's professional development to show an interest in what's going on. Stepping out to meet with the other principals is a way to collaborate, but it's not something the teachers had the opportunity to do. Hanging out with peers could easily be seen as administrative privilege.

Mr. Blighton should meet individually with each of the teachers regarding their forged professional development sheets, noting that the meeting would be documented. Additionally, he could assign a brief follow-up, such as asking the teachers to write a summary of each session's main points.

The social media comments are more serious. Unless there is a policy prohibiting the use of social media during work hours, teachers may have felt they could message each other. The content, however, was inappropriate, and the district's accepted-use policy should clearly mention that no employee may speak or write negatively of another in social media.

To improve the annual professional development for all employees, the principals could get together to stress to the superintendent the importance of teacher collaboration. Failing that, they can organize sessions across their own campuses. They should also encourage the district to digitize some of their procedures, such as attendance verification.

If the originator of the meme can be identified, that employee may be subject to disciplinary action.

Resolution to Don't Drink the Water Case Study

Grade Level: Rural Elementary School, Grades PK–5
Standards: 7b, c, d, Professional Community for Teachers and Staff

The school nurse should not have taken it upon herself to label every drinking fountain as contaminated. It would have been better to first call the principal at the meeting. He could have had each water fountain unplugged and have bottled water delivered to each classroom. Then he could have sent a letter home informing parents that, due to concerns about the water, they turned off the water fountains and every classroom had plenty of bottled water to drink instead.

Possible options included removing the water fountain signs, alerting the custodians to disconnect the fountains, or having someone take phone messages until his return. Going in the back door suggests that the principal had something to hide.

Mr. Huston should tell the nurse that he'd like a copy of the data she used to make her determination. She should not have taken the initiative to label the water conditions without conclusive evidence and permission to do so. This should be in a warning, with written documentation, that a verbal warning has been given.

Mr. Huston could have avoided the situation had he listened to his nurse that morning. Now Mr. Huston will have to assure the parents that the water is fine, possibly by having it tested or by acquiring a statement from the water supply company. He should also address any misstatements made on social media. He may send a letter home with the students; he must call the superintendent regarding the outcome.

Resolution to Where's My Kid? Case Study

Grade Level: Rural Elementary School, Grades PK–5
Standards: 8j, Meaningful Engagement of Families and Community; 10a, School Improvement

Ms. Hernandez has every right to not allow Ms. Tucker to film and publicize who the illegal immigrants may be. Although Ms. Tucker has the right to freedom of speech through the First Amendment, she does not have the right to infringe on the rights of others. She must abide by school policy, and in the absence of a written policy, the principal is the voice for campus policy.

Most states have laws prohibiting the exclusion of illegal aliens in the school systems, asserting that the Equal Protection Clause allows their enrollment. Under the Fourteenth Amendment, anyone in the state is subject to the laws of said state. This case was pleaded and won in Texas (*Plyler v. Doe* No. 80-1538) in 1982, and it has become a landmark decision.

Children whose parents do not live in the United States and cross the border daily to drop a child off at school may not be subject to the laws of the state because they do not reside in the state.

Protective services may remove children from the school without parent permission. It is advisable to photocopy the person's driver's license and any other documentation of their identity.

Ms. Hernandez should relay this information to the parent, explaining that this rule exists outside the school's jurisdiction and the school must follow it.

Resolution to When Push Comes to Shove Case Study

Grade Level: Suburban Elementary School, Grades PK–5
Standards: 8a, b, Meaningful Engagement of Families and Community

The principal's first response should be to take care of the injured child. She or the nurse can call the parents to let them know what has happened and that the nurse is recommending that the child get stitches.

It is the principal's job to tell Peter's parents that he is one of several bullies in the classroom, and because of the district's policy, he will face consequences for his actions. Mrs. Russ must also call Mary's parents to report that their daughter assaulted another student, causing bodily harm. She, too, will face consequences for her actions. In most school districts, the students would be facing suspension.

The next step is to follow up with Mrs. Dinsley. Mrs. Russ can ask for a written statement of what happened. Mrs. Russ should make it clear that any bullying incidents are to be taken seriously and reported immediately.

Mrs. Russ failed to follow through with several things. First, she forgot to check on Mary in the classroom and didn't even meet with her until several days later. Mrs. Russ also accepted Mrs. Dinsley's statement as truthful, without verifying its validity. Finally, Mrs. Russ did not meet with the alleged bullies and hand out consequences to them.

About the Author

Wafa Hozien's professional background includes over twenty years' work as a high school history teacher and a school administrator. She has designed and delivered training for school districts, universities, and leadership academies throughout the United States and internationally and specializes in combining research-based strategies and practical applications, then working with school administrators, teacher leaders, and school districts to adopt innovative strategies for their locations. Specifically, she values the incorporation of issues related to culture, ethnicity, race, and religion in the education process.

Dr. Hozien has published numerous articles and publications on diversity issues in education. To help reduce inequities in education, she makes herself available by educating through interactive workshops at schools, community organizations, and campus lectures on cultural competency and social justice. She has been researching the experiences of minority adolescent girls' public schooling experiences. In the multicultural education context, she has published and presented at workshops and conferences on minority student experiences.

Dr. Hozien is assistant professor of educational leadership at Central Michigan University, where she teaches graduate students in the principal and superintendent doctoral preparation programs. Social justice, nondiscrimination, and equality are key principles that Dr. Hozien applies to education in all of the courses she teaches at Central Michigan University.

Dr. Hozien appreciates constructive feedback and gaining insight into best practices and ways to improve this book. If you find that this book is missing something or have suggestions for improvement, then kindly contact her via e-mail at whozien@gmail.com.

Her most recent book is *SLLA Crash Course: Approaches for Success* (2017, Rowman and Littlefield).